Lessons Learned at the Shore

A JOURNEY THROUGH RETIREMENT

Roy Laux

Synergy Group
WHITE OAK, PENNSYLVANIA

Roy Laux/Synergy Group
The Synergy Group
1967 Lincoln Way
White Oak, PA 15131
www.synergygroupinc.com
Book layout ©2012 BookDesignTemplates.com

Lessons Learned at the Shore/ Roy Laux. —1st ed.
ISBN 9781092595292

Contents

This book is dedicated to Cindy, who makes every day even more special than the beach.

Hug the shore, let others try the deep.

—VIRGIL

Preface

Financial planning can be complicated. Retirement planning takes that challenge to a whole new level. A retirement journey takes you through the rough lands of market volatility, taxation, inflation, long-term care risks, and many other potential roadblocks that can truly wreck a retirement.

Lessons Learned at the Shore takes all of those challenges and attacks them one by one, in a simple yet effectively informative manner. Taking understandable analogies and weaving them together to explain the key areas we will all face in our golden years will allow you to not only understand the challenges you face in retirement, but how to deal with them head on.

I can't fathom anyone who knows how to combine a love for the shore and all of its pleasantries with a career spent helping people achieve their retirement goals like my father. After his faith and his family, Roy's passion for helping retirees achieve their goals, combined with his love for the beach, has created the perfect blend for this book. I not only have hands-on experience as my father mentored me as a retirement advisor, but I've seen him provide the roadmap for so many families in their financial lives.

If you are planning to retire soon or are already retired, allow the pages of this book to be the guide in your personal retirement journey. Allow the lessons Roy has learned over his lifetime of helping people work towards a predictable retirement make your retirement more effective and simpler. And for those that share Roy's love of the shore, allow the book to stir up the family memories you have from the beach and bring you back to those times when life was more relaxed and simpler, as well.

~Jason Laux,
Vice President
Synergy Financial Group

Introduction

So, what does the beach have to do with retirement planning? For almost fifty years now, I have vacationed, relaxed, and just plain old enjoyed a considerable amount of time down at the Jersey Shore. Our family has travelled there for our annual vacations and later purchased a condo there. We have sought refreshment and relaxation in this spot because it is different from home but is still close enough to be comfortably accessible.

I always get excited when I see the Wildwood Beach sign: it's a sign I'm about to make long-lasting memories.

That's not to say that I haven't seen beaches elsewhere, and certainly some with very much more of a "wow" factor people often remark on. Yet, the times spent at Wildwood have left an indelible mark on me and provided me considerable life lessons, lessons that I feel are applicable to my life in many ways. Life's lessons are learned in many ways, some of which take a lifetime to absorb. For me, I can sense the wonders of nature and feel the power of God with each new wave crashing on shore, all the while experiencing a soothing of the worries and pressures of life as they are washed away, wave by wave. Like a snowflake, each wave provides a unique lesson that can provide insight to many areas of life.

Those who know me know I am always looking for unique connection opportunities, putting together thoughts and ideas not always readily connected. Which brings us around to the central topic of this book. As I stated, the beach has provided me with many life lessons, including those that translate into lessons about retirement. So, in these pages, I intend to take some of the lessons that I've learned over the past five decades from the beach and apply them to the retirement planning techniques I have taught over the past thirty-plus years. I trust you will find this work refreshing as well as entertaining and perhaps, just perhaps, insightful as well.

As I first took the opportunity to put down on paper some of the things I've learned since 1984, the year that I entered this industry, I thought it might be beneficial for those who get an opportunity to read this to perhaps hear a different perspective. My motivation here is not to tell you what to think or why to think it. Instead, I hope to explain why people in our industry strategize in certain approaches to financial preparation. I also hope to reveal to you that sometimes, in doing so, different financial professionals perhaps turn a blind eye to other solutions that might exist outside of their specialty. I think doing so can be detrimental to the overall ability to craft a retirement portfolio. Please understand—since most of my life's work has been devoted to helping people prepare for retirement—this work is purely about retirement planning.

So, let's start out with defining what a successful retirement financial plan looks like. I would like to note that this perspective represents a very conservative posture and very much reflects my personal positions on the matter. For me, first and foremost, it includes an income plan. You must develop a budget (sorry, Cindy. My wife despises that word) and, once you've established, funded, and put it in place, your focus can shift in the direction of the arena of opportunities and you can look to whatever products and services are acceptable to you based on your goals and circumstances.

You can't help but feel content when you look out across the Wildwood sky. It's similar to the feeling of a satisfying, adequate retirement plan.

My definition of financial success in retirement is simply this if you're able to achieve the things in retirement that you desire (joy expenses) as well as those that are required (food, shelter taxes, etc.). If you can fund those and do so without running out of cash before running out of financial breath, you have achieved a successful retirement in my book. Sure, we can get into legacy and tax planning in the retirement discussion, but if you have what you must and some of what you desire (hopefully lots of what you desire) and don't run out of cash before you and your spouse head on to higher grounds, your mission is accomplished.

I won't be asking you to agree with me on all points as you read this, although for the life of me, I don't know why you wouldn't. However, I *will* ask that you have an open mind and perhaps, at the end of the book, you will have determined that a few other possibilities exist beyond the single path that you may have undertaken, whether you took that path through purposeful decision or by default. Just as the friends we have made down at the shore would never root for a Steeler or Penguin team (you take your life into your hands wearing a Pittsburgh team jersey!), don't let yourself be peer-pressured into your retirement plan.

I hope you enjoy this book, and perhaps someday you and I will be able to actually have an open, in-person discussion about your retirement. If you have listened to our weekly radio shows, you know we always stress how so many areas of life are much more important than financial planning. We invariably close with some comments on the importance of spending time with your family and the undeniable value of spending time connecting with God. I encourage you to do the best planning you possibly can, but remember it is God who ultimately provides.

CHAPTER ONE

But I Need, No, I *Deserve* a Vacation!

A basic assumption I will make here is that, if you are reading this, you are close to or in retirement and attempting to deal with all that retirement planning brings to the table, which is way more than just money. So, as we begin, allow me to ask you a few questions. Let's start by planning a trip to the shore.

Do you remember when you and some buddies first got an itch for a road trip? In the early years the packing and planning was pretty simple. Someone suggested the trip and an hour later you threw some clothes in a bag and some cash in your pocket, hopped in the car, and hit the beach. This is much like the early years of our careers. when we first entered the workforce, we gave little thought to the details of what our retirement would look like. Perhaps there was a 401(k) plan there at work and that was great. Unfortunately for so many, the thought was, "What's the least I can put in to get the company match? Can someone put that money into some sort of investment for me? Because I just don't have the focus to work on something I won't use for forty-five years."

Every time we arrive in Wildwood, I am excited to see the big welcome sign. It makes me feel like I have arrived home.

But what a difference some planning could make. Perhaps this wisdom is not for you but is something you hope to impart on to your kids.

If this is your plan, sit them down, lock the door, and tell them how much your wish for them to be smarter than you were and what a difference it could make if they simply would engage in some good planning. Just like putting on sunscreen at twenty-five helps prevent skin cancer at sixty-five, perhaps understanding why funding a Roth option in the 401(k) could result in perhaps a sizeable nest egg of tax-free money when retiring. Get specific and discuss what makes the difference in funding an amazing retirement. Help your younger relatives learn that, just like sunscreen, retirement planning is best applied early and often.

As we travel through this journey called life, we are challenged to face each new chapter and deal with all that it brought to our door. Tell me that life isn't like a giant sieve on potential retirement savings! Finding the perfect match to walk through life with is certainly a different challenge than merely finding the best-looking among the goddesses in bathing suits on the shore, or simply getting a date for dinner. Wooing someone who will be your partner in thick and thin, then raising kids, buying a house, and funding family vacations takes precedence over putting the max into the retirement plan.

No matter what the issue is, it usually takes precedence over saving for a future retirement need that is seemingly miles and miles down the highway. Did you ever notice how a day can seem to last a month while twenty years has rushed by, seemingly in a flash? Retirement is sometimes like that—it may seem a distance away, but one day you will wake up and the needs required for a successful retirement will be hard upon you.

Sometimes the necessities of life are so pressing that we can't see the way clear enough to add to the retirement plan at all. After all, the kids deserve that trip to the beach this year, and that retirement thing is years down the road. It's called life, and in the 15,340 ½ days that your forty-two years of working includes, it seems each one will provide some need more critical, more important (and more fun) than saving for retirement. At least until somewhere around age fifty-eight (insert your age of choice here, but I observe a change in mindset typically in the mid-to-late-fifties) when you come to realize that there may be a tsunami headed for the very beach you are walking on.

A sense of reality sets in as you start to do the math and realize that your savings are just as empty as a Jersey Beach when late fall steals the last warmth from the ocean. Perhaps a lack of planning has stolen your retirement dreams. If that is where you're at, if you are feeling the pain of past sunburns, do something about it! Eliminate debt. Increase savings and build a plan during those last few working years before retirement. Doing that can help provide some predictability into your retirement future. Start today and do it with your spouse as a team and consider adding the talents of a retirement planner to that team, as well.

For some, the preceding is their reality, and there will be fewer beach trips in retirement than what they desired. But others took a different path, proceeding with thoughtful action to be able to include beautiful sunsets over the water deep into their retirement years. In this case, my beach metaphor is simply a stand-in for whatever you envision for your retirement. Successfully saving enough to have many visits to the beach in this case is just to say that your dream for you and your family perhaps is now possible.

What a wonderful awakening occurs as I sit with a couple who diligently prepared for that day when the paycheck from work is replaced with the one crafted from their 401(k) and they are confident they can make the retirement they planned a reality. They can do that because of the years of savings they built into their plans and because together we have structured their retirement income plan. They have crafted and put in place a budget that includes their "joy" expenses as well as needs, and it is fully funded. They've structured their assets to account for their own lifestyle expectations, giving themselves their own income that accounts for inflation. All their savings are about ready to pay off, as they have forward-funded their own futures.

You know better than anyone which path has brought you to where you are today. If it is the first example and there is work to do, don't give up yet! Roll up your sleeves and together let's get to work to do everything possible to get back on track. You might be amazed at what you may still accomplish.

Just like retirement planning, the whack-a-mole game my grand-kids love to play requires a lot of intense, dedicated focus.

If you are in the second group, congratulations! Now the transition begins as you learn the differences between building a retirement fund and wisely using those funds to generate lifetime, inflation-adjusted income. This is the point where you begin to understand the difference between yield and growth, and why maximizing that knowledge can add predictability and stability to the walk through this retirement journey. Hopefully, it will also be a time of developing an awareness of why pairing up with an experienced retirement advisor will also be valuable, as your journey now has a different focus. I welcome the opportunity to discuss that path with you as you traverse a new venture in life.

CHAPTER TWO

Off-Season Planning

Perhaps you are retiring and have been using a variety of investment products, including mutual funds, bonds, exchange-traded funds, etc. in your 401(k). As far as you can see, that makes sense going forward, right? Perhaps not.

Did you ever notice that a trip to the beach costs less depending on the season? Perhaps you realized there are other benefits to off-season travel as well. Go to the Wildwood Beach in July and it is insane. Everyone from Philly to New York and as far as parts of Canada have rented every room—every inch of space. Crowds swell the lines at every restaurant and the wait can be hours long. Cars are parked in every available parking space in town—a particular pet peeve of mine. The water and amusement parks are packed, as well. Literally hundreds of thousands of vacationers are trying to soak up every last ray of sun, every ocean breeze, to get the most from those vacation dollars. Those who live on the Island year-round moan about traffic and the congestion, but many are employed for the very reason that they are frustrated.

When some hit retirement, many advisors continue to invest their dollars as if they were still at work. They position their assets as though their clients are still adding to the accounts as opposed to spending them. If you were this client, your advisor invests your money as if you were going to the beach in prime season. Just following the crowd, as it were. Sure, they might suggest that you add a bit more of a conservative posture (read as possibly "add some bonds") as you age, but the plan is often still fully dependent on market performance to achieve results.

In these cases, an advisor who is growth-focused typically gives little thought to the idea that creating a monthly income from the account might just require a different kind of plan. They may not consider that the risk associated with a market correction, particularly when combined with a person's need to draw income, maybe an insurmountable wave to ride for those who are in or near retirement. Perhaps retirement planning is like planning for an off-season beach trip, requiring a different strategy than what you would use if you are just following the crowd. In part, it is about learning the difference between that which is in your control as opposed to that which is not, and how to work within that given frame.

This picture was taken during an off-season trip to Wildwood beach. As you can see, all of us still had a ton of fun!

September and October trips to the shore mean dwindling crowds, discounted rooms, warm water, and sunny days. Once discovered, off-season trips become very attractive for those who are looking for a better way, a different strategy. Sure, off-season beach trips aren't for everyone. Anyone who is in school or has children in school may find fall travel to be nearly impossible. This may limit fall trips more to those who are later in life (similar to retirement). Magazines and store racks are quick to remind us that aging sometimes has some frailties, but I'd encourage you not to overlook its amazing perks. Take advantage of the benefits that this time of life can provide.

Off-Season Retirement Planning: A Definition

Let's define our off-season retirement planning. Chiefly, I mean off-season retirement planning to mean that we aren't following the crowds by exposing ourselves to unnecessary market turbulence. Instead, we are minimizing exposure to market losses. That discounted room rate equates to "lifetime income guarantees" (available from certain annuity products with guarantees based on the claims paying ability of the chosen insurance company) and warm and sunny days translate to the peace of mind that adding predictability and steadiness to your income can provide. Let's eliminate the angst—the frustration of standing in line for an hour-and-a-half to be seated at your favorite restaurant—and replace it with a guaranteed seat at the lifetime income table,[1] thereby eliminating the fear of outliving your money. Numerous surveys list running out of money as today's number one concern of mature Americans.[2]

---

[1] Guaranteed life income can be provided by certain annuity products. The guarantees associated are based on the claims-paying ability of the issuing insurance company

[2] TransAmerica Center for Retirement Studies. August 2016. "Perspectives on Retirement: Baby Boomers, Generation X, and Millennials."

With proper planning, you can address this issue and a put in place a much more predictable path. If, as I suggest, you address and manage this issue now, you can then focus on other matters, such as to which beach you might most want to travel.

Let's do that by doing some "off-season," retirement-oriented planning as early as possible. In many ways, retirement is the off-season time of our lives. We are officially off the clock, and while we are still very much involved in life, it is a different season, a different time in our lives.

Instead of focusing on pooling our money into market-based investments, we are now looking at what to do with the money we have saved in our 401(k) or IRA or other investment. We are considering what products we should turn to in order to first fill income needs, and then and only then will we think of investment vehicles. The way this comes about for you will be different than it is for someone else—your needs and goals are different, and thus your strategy will be, too. This may seem like a somewhat daunting task. I find the best approach is to begin by putting all financial products on the table for an open and honest discussion of the weaknesses and strengths of each.

Efficiency in Your Planning

Perhaps we could plan this financial "off-season" retirement trip in a fashion designed to maximize the opportunities life now provides using financial tools that are well designed for the trip. Did you realize that, for many, once you reach age fifty-nine-and-one-half, you have options for your retirement accounts even while you are still employed? Of course, it depends on your employer, but you may have the option to move your qualified employer-sponsored

https://www.transamericacenter.org/docs/default-source/retirement-survey-of-workers/tcrs2016_sr_perspectives_on_retirement_baby_boomers_genx_millennials.pdf retirement plans, such 401(k) or 403(b), to an IRA of your choice. It's called an "in-service distribution" and could be something you benefit from. In-service distributions are subject to the specific provisions of each employer's plan documents and may include restrictions which could vary based on the source (e.g., employee deferrals, profit sharing) and are generally based on factors such as age and service.

An advantage of moving funds over to an IRA is about efficiency—particularly if you have IRAs from other employers or are looking to explore a Roth option. Yet one retirement account may have a better selection of investments or lesser fees, so work with a financial professional to decide what is best for your circumstances. The bottom line is that if we strive to maximize the efficiency of each part of your assets while also analyzing the way it all works together, perhaps we can minimize some of the risks. If we find enough efficiencies (cutting out unnecessary fees, unnecessary taxes, or unintentional investments), it may allow us to keep more assets in conservative vehicles—perhaps we can stay out of the financial waters when riptides are present and reduce any unnecessary risks.

When you are young and time is on your side, risk is more of an adventure (like your youth when you could take the risk of missing out on hotel rooms at the beach). But when you are looking at relying on your retirement savings for income (or when you are an older vacationer taking along your family to your beach trip), risks in retirement portfolios are not always your friend and you should consider if the risk is absolutely necessary.

Although these kites are in the air now, eventually they will come down. Your investments are similar: what if the wind isn't blowing hard enough to keep your finances in the air?

Investing Does Not Equal Income

To be clear, you cannot stick your head in the sand at the expense of growth potential. However, we teach that the risks associated with vehicles offering market growth potential should only be linked with retirement funds not allocated to income needs. This means that, while you should probably have a portion of your assets invested in market-based vehicles for growth potential, the products from which you draw your income, or your paycheck, in retirement should not have their principal subject to the unpredictable whims of the market.

Can you see the value in this planning strategy? If the market were to have a significant correction and that correction did not have an impact on your budget, would that make you more comfortable in simply knowing that fact? Obviously, the market-based portion of your assets was impacted, but not the assets you depend on for day-to-day living expenses. The market-linked portion of your retirement savings will have the opportunity and time to recover along with the market while the necessities of life continue to be provided for.

This approach of establishing a paycheck through non-market-based products is what I consider to be off-season retirement planning and, in my opinion, far too few advisors incorporate this strategy, which is to allocate the investment into specific products for the specific need. In my practice, when we talk about products with market-based growth potential, we mean tools like mutual funds, stocks, ETFs, bonds, and the like. These products involve risk of losing money in the short term, but they are also the ones with the most potential to gain in the long term.

Income-generating products mean annuities. Some advisors like to turn to a single product to meet all needs, but that often causes inefficiency. Like a shop on the boardwalk that tries to be all things to all people, it ends up being too much and too little all at once. Instead, we should look at products individually to suit each need. You'll need products that can outpace inflation and provide funds for that need in the future—even if that means dealing with the risk of loss in the market. You'll need products to address increased medical costs that occur in greater frequency later in life, as well. If you are interested in legacy planning and tax efficiency, you'll want to consider your products in light of those needs. Once you have identified your need (what you are asking those dollars to do) it will quickly lead you to the path that identifies the product for that specific job. Don't be afraid to consider all financial products as viable as long as they answer the question, "is this product suitable for this need?"

The off-season retirement portfolio has many advantages. Just like off-season vacations, off-season retirement planning has a uniqueness that would have not been appropriate while working and growing your retirement savings. However, once the concept of focusing on income and yield replaces the goal of simply growing, things sharply come into focus.

Now instead of going to the shore in July, we go in late September and experience fewer crowds. Now we seek less volatility in our investments. Now instead of inflated in-season rates we look for nice discounts. In retirement we can and should seek to lower fees and risks in our portfolio, all while providing for the needs and desires we seek, as well. Every season in life is unique and requires adjustments to facilitate future needs, which will be different than past experiences.

During this off-season trip, our family seemed to have Wildwood beach all to ourselves.

An off-season trip does not mean less enjoyment, and off-season retirement planning does not mean being able to do less. It means knowing what you *can* do and providing for a full future.

I have heard the retirement sequence described as moving through the go-go years, to the slow-go years, to the no-go years. Each has its own ramifications. I believe the off-season years deserve front-end funding as much as possible to allow you to experience the go-go years to the max. Crafting a retirement plan that includes this strategy, in my opinion, would be a wonderful discussion to have with your retirement advisor. Perhaps with me.

CHAPTER THREE

Stormy Weather

Having owned a condo on the Wildwood Beach for almost twenty years now, we have experienced the full range of what the ocean weather looks like. Obviously, when the days are warm and sunny and the waters glisten with the reflections of the of the blue skies and radiance of the sun, there are few places I would rather be. Sun-filled skies, warm sand, and gentle waves make for some amazing, relaxing times. As summer deepens and the waters warm up, life just keeps getting better and better. But wait. The very warmth that provides comfort can be the catalyst of future volatility.

Storms are different at the beach than they are back in Pittsburgh. Some are more likely to occur in spring and late fall as the weather patterns sometimes develop into what is called a Nor'easter. It is a miserable period of two to four days when a circular pattern of wind and rain settle in and just won't let go. The beach and roadways flood. There is just nowhere for all that water to go. The tides push the water in all the further, and for those days, those three or four days that seem like a month, the beach is a wet, dreary place to be. Experience teaches us these storms will pass.

Emotionally, these days can be draining. In times of emotional strain, we sometimes take actions that are not in our best interests.

When rough weather hits, the beach is deserted. Don't allow financial storms to empty your retirement funds.

Nor'easters of Finance

Financial storms in your retirement years sometimes take on the characteristics of a Nor'easter. Something somewhere will trigger a short-term market period of volatility and, just like the emotional drain from a weather pattern, sometimes we react emotionally in a way that is harmful. It is wise to not trade on the headlines, but to remain disciplined through the storms. An experienced advisor may be the protection from these emotional tendencies we all experience (most frequently with poor results).

Let's consider an example. Go back a few years to the time when so much discussion in the financial world centered on what was occurring in Greece. As the headlines continued, the financial markets reacted. In a relatively short two- to three-week period, our market quickly fell, then leveled off. The storm passed, the ship righted itself, and the market rebounded back to where it was. The financial Nor'easter hit, did its damage, and then passed.

Here, my grandson, Tyler, drives his go-cart in a twisting fashion, like the Nor'easter that might hit us later in the evening.

For many, it created a problem that financially went far beyond those two or three weeks. If the emotional strain that market cycle created caused you to bail out on the way down, you likely experienced a loss when you reinvested a few months later. I mean no disrespect, but in reality, what did the mess that Greece was experiencing actually mean to our markets? Had it not been for the desire to sell newspapers or bump up the evening news ratings, would it really have been the global economic tragedy it was made out to be? It certainly was a significant, gut-wrenching ordeal if you lived in Greece, but come on, it did not—it could not—have the effect on our economy it was portrayed to have the potential to cause.

Perhaps in your own portfolio you can recall some similar emotional event where you suffered adversely from an emotional financial decision. Perhaps having a good ally, a coach if you will, on your team would have made a difference. Perhaps having a retirement coach on your team would be wise at this new juncture of your financial life to help prevent these knee-jerk reactions in the future.

Storm Lessons: Sequence of Returns Risk
(Or, What Happens First)

Two very important retirement lessons here. First, consider the wisdom of separating the portion of your investments designated to provide income (budget expenses) from market-based products. Let me take a moment here to discuss a concept known as "sequence of returns risk."

When you are investing for the long-term, you are exposing your assets to market risk. This is an accepted part of investing; nothing ventured, nothing gained. The market may experience gains, and it may experience losses. Yet, when you begin withdrawing money from those investments, the order in which those gains and losses happen becomes very important. A big loss early in retirement can mean the difference in possibly running out of money, while a big loss later in retirement may not have as much impact.

On the following pages, you'll see a simple illustration of this mathematical concept. Both charts feature the same market losses, the same starting investment, and the same, steady $5,000 withdrawal in each year. Yet, after twenty years, one of them is at a third of its original value while the other has actually increased in value. The difference? One began its withdrawals with three years of losses. The second chart has the same market activity, but it has been reversed—the three years in a row of market losses happen at the end of the twenty years for this portfolio.

Sequence of Returns—Losses Early

Investment	Market	Withdrawal
$100,000	-2.93%	-$5,000
$92,070.00	-5.95%	-$5,000
$81,591.84	-11.42%	-$5,000
$67,274.05	15.97%	-$5,000
$73,017.71	5.63%	-$5,000
$72,128.61	1.27%	-$5,000
$68,044.64	8.40%	-$5,000
$68,760.39	3.41%	-$5,000
$66,105.12	-22.50%	-$5,000
$46,231.47	14.94%	-$5,000
$48,138.45	8.78%	-$5,000
$47,365.01	1.64%	-$5,000
$43,141.79	8.23%	-$5,000
$41,692.36	15.45%	-$5,000
$43,133.83	7.72%	-$5,000
$41,463.77	-1.72%	-$5,000
$35,750.59	5.28%	-$5,000
$32,638.22	20.97%	-$5,000
$34,482.46	17.98%	-$5,000
$35,682.40	9.89%	-$5,000
$34,211.39		

Sequence of Returns—Reversed

Investment	Market	With-drawal
$100,000	9.89%	-$5,000
$104,890.00	17.98%	-$5,000
$118,749.22	20.97%	-$5,000
$138,650.93	5.28%	-$5,000
$140,971.70	-1.72%	-$5,000
$133,546.99	7.72%	-$5,000
$138,856.82	15.45%	-$5,000
$155,310.20	8.23%	-$5,000
$163,092.22	1.64%	-$5,000
$160,766.94	8.78%	-$5,000
$169,882.27	14.94%	-$5,000
$190,262.69	-22.50%	-$5,000
$142,453.58	3.41%	-$5,000
$142,311.25	8.40%	-$5,000
$149,265.39	1.27%	-$5,000
$146,161.06	5.63%	-$5,000
$149,389.93	15.97%	-$5,000
$168,247.50	-11.42%	-$5,000
$144,033.64	-5.95%	-$5,000
$130,463.64	-2.93%	-$5,000
$121,641.05		

Now again, this is hypothetical, but even without taxes and fees I think this shows what the concept of "sequence of returns" means to a retirement plan. You can see how withdrawing monthly income coupled with significant market drops can torpedo your retirement security.

Think of the city as the market. Often it looks fine when you look at it from afar, but if you zoom into one of the windows and see an individual's situation, things might not look so positive.

If you intend to base your retirement income needs on market-based products, this is a lesson you need to understand. The financial markets have historically provided strong opportunities for growth and are without doubt an important piece of the retirement plan. At the same time, those same markets have been through economic storms. While the markets have recovered each time overall, individual investments haven't fared as well. In my opinion, we shouldn't seek to generate income when the market experiences the storms it sometimes brings.

Storm Lessons: Navigating in the Storm (Or, Does Your Compass Point North?)

The second lesson is to consider the value of working with a retirement professional who, if they do their job properly, should help to reduce or eliminate as much as possible the emotional reactions we are all prone to have. Trading off headlines is a recipe for retirement failure (i.e. running out of money while still breathing). A good ally—a good retirement advisor—should be able to help you to weather the storm by helping remove the emotional component as much as possible from the actions you make regarding your investments. If, as we teach, your income dollars are not in market-based positions, then the storm doesn't touch you. These market-based products are positioned for growth opportunities, but are also exposed to the potential for loss.

This is a lesson unique to retirement—it is a very different approach from what we used and trusted during the decades in which we were building our accounts. The day you begin drawing income from those retirement savings is the day everything changes.

Sometimes storms at the beach are much more severe and do much more damage than a Nor'easter. Sometimes the warm waters and the wonderful heat of the summer season allows for much more powerful and potentially life-threatening storms to hit. Sometimes hurricanes happen. Because Wildwood is so far north, the storms usually soften up by the time they reach the beach.

But occasionally a Hurricane Sandy will hit. And when it does you had better have done all you can to prepare. The winds and rain are relentless. The flooding destroys property and takes lives. There is nowhere to hide.

Sandy hit about twenty miles up the coast, and those towns north of Wildwood were hit harder than Wildwood. But as close as the center of that monster was, significant damage was unavoidable. Sometimes in life, as with storms, it is the secondary wave that causes the most damage. The flooding usually hits after the real storm has seemingly passed. This flooding results from the massive amounts of rain or the tornados that spin off because of the disruption in the atmosphere. It can cause even more significant problems than the original storm.

In the past twenty or so years, we have had great growth as well as many storms in the financial market. Two would, in my opinion, go down as category five hurricanes: the financial catastrophes that occurred in 2001 following 9/11 and the Great Recession of 2008.

When I discuss retirement planning with my clients, I often refer to these two "hurricanes." In my opinion, both 2001 and 2008 were times when normal market corrections were probably due, but in both instances the market drops were pushed far deeper in strength by outside influences. When people fly planes into buildings, normalcy has no chance. When our government allows our banks and financial institutions to be unregulated to the degree we saw, it was lucky we survived that financial mess at all. The storms' effects, worsened by the actions of others in both of these examples, could not be mitigated without having planned in advance for how to recover from the damage. Sound retirement planning is designed to deal with not only the primary storms but the secondary storms that may follow closely behind, as well.

These financial hurricanes were devastating to many retirees, particularly those following the 4 percent rule or some other purely market-based withdrawal strategy to fund their retirement.

The Four Percent Rule

The 4 percent rule was developed in the 1990s (during the tech stock run, before the bubble burst), and it theorized that a portfolio that was well-diversified with stocks and bonds could stand for an investor to withdraw up to 4 percent of the account value per year, increasing each year to address inflation.[3]

Of course, this was prior to the Great Recession, and was based off a time when retirement didn't last as long as it does, with people retiring earlier and living longer than before.

For this very reason, myself and others at our firm strongly counsel to separate income dollars from the market, and to invest only money for future needs to "market-based" investments, which can offer the opportunity for growth (as well as exposure to market loss). As we teach these lessons in our classes at the local colleges, it is exciting for me to sense the awareness of those attending as they realize the wisdom in this basic lesson and hopefully implement some of those lessons into their overall plans as well.

Consider the results of using this strategy. What would happen if, when the twin towers fell and then the market dropped just as fast? If your income was not based on market-oriented investments, your income would not have been one cent lower. Your growth account would have been affected, as it was market-based, but not your income. Your fixed expenses and the budgeted joy expenses would be still arriving day by day, month by month, just like one wave follows the next on the beach.

You are less likely to respond to a financial hurricane with a strong emotional reaction if your income isn't subject to the market, because you would understand that, while the storm hit, you

---

[3] Julia Kagan. Investopedia. February 7, 2019. "The Four Percent Rule." https://www.investopedia.com/terms/f/four-percent-rule.asp

were prepared. Also, without having to be drained in a downturn by consistent income withdrawals, your market-based funds would also have more time in which to recover from the financial turbulence. This provides time in which we could hope your market-based assets might recover and maybe even keep up with or even outstrip inflation.

I personally plan for my retirement with my legacy in mind. When I consider how my retirement funds will affect my children and grandchildren, I am motivated to be patient and save everything I can for them.

This is the hope and the goal of solid retirement-oriented planning. This predictability is what solid conservative planning strives to bring to the table. How does this compare to what you experienced earlier in the millennium? What could you expect from it tomorrow if some similar storm were to strike? Have you made solid, intelligent changes to your investment portfolio to deal with what the hurricanes of life will bring to your retirement needs? If not, perhaps now is the perfect time, while the weather is calm, to do so. I would be honored to be to help in this area.

CHAPTER FOUR

Pizza, Fries, and Hot Sausage Sandwiches with Peppers and Onions

One thing is for shore (pardon the pun), when it comes to things to eat, it's darn hard to beat the Wildwood Boardwalk. Two miles of nothing but eateries, games, t-shirt shops, water parks, and amusement rides. Every kid's dream, even when the kid is a white-haired sixty-six-year-old looking to extend his youth.

The art of the Boardwalk when it comes to food is, over the years, to slowly and skillfully sharpen your taste buds, thereby being able to discern the best the Boards have to offer. Not that other quality choices don't exist, but it's important to find the perfect lineup for you. From all the products to choose from, which pizza is a cut above? Whose sandwich roll offers just the right chewiness to hold up to the sausage sandwich until that last bite is popped into your mouth and the clock begins ticking down for the next dietary adventure to come into sight?

The Hot Spot serves the best sausage, pepper, and onion sandwich in Wildwood.

For me, the list is Sam's for pepperoni; Mack's for a slice of white; the Hot Spot for a sausage, pepper, and onions; and Curley's for fries. There it is: the culinary list it took me forty-six years to refine. The product choices span the length of the Boards and will appease the most educated palate. Obviously, the list goes on when adding sweet choices like Italian ice (cherry flavor at Hershey's) or vanilla fudge (Douglass's), but you can't go wrong with my top four product choices.

So how do pizza, fries, and sandwiches fit into a retirement discussion? Assuming you're not at the Wildwood Boardwalk (but if you are, stop reading and go grab a slice!), here we go.

Sam's: my go-to pizza place. My favorite topping is pepperoni.

In retirement we must choose the products we will purchase with our 401(k), IRA, or other retirement account to provide the income we will need when these funds become the source of our monthly income. When the paycheck from the employer is no longer there, you will be changing the focus of what your funds are tasked to do. The overarching goal of growth, over all else, must be now coupled with the need for income. Income must be structured to last, and for married folks it must stretch for two lifetimes. What worked before to achieve the desired growth must now shift in focus to maintain income—which is king in retirement. I defy you to retire without adequate lifetime income. Can't happen—or at least not in a way that anyone would characterize as a "successful" or desirable retirement. In life as we age, our digestive systems sometimes show the signs of that aging as well. What never caused any gastronomic distress now does. In retirement, the same logic applies. The strategies we used before sometimes need editing.

I have been visiting restaurants on the Wildwood boardwalk for years now, and only recently have I developed the perfect culinary menu for myself. You might prefer other places. We are all different in terms of taste, as well as retirement needs and goals.

For some, the path will change little. The same products that got them there, all market-based, will be tweaked a bit and the dice will be rolled to carry them through retirement This is in part because that may be all their pre-retirement advisor understands. I do, however, question the wisdom here. Many of us seek out the counsel of specialists when a medical need arises, so why do we not seek out an experienced retirement counselor as we walk through this new stage of life? Adding a pro to your team who understands the nuances of retirement planning and who brings legal, insurance, and CPA professionals to the mix can be comforting and efficient at this stage of life.

Here at Synergy Group, we have a team that includes in-office professionals from different backgrounds, and also extends to a network of referring professionals. Instead of having all the pieces of a plan working independently of each other, we choose a different plan of action for our clients. We choose to plan in a retirement-oriented way that provides a predictable strategy to the path of lifetime income, and which is efficient for tax and estate planning.

Shifting Gears for Retirement

In the classes we teach at Pitt, Penn State, and CCAC, we unfold a product strategy that shifts the focus from chasing growth potential to putting income first (of course there is still an element of growth potential, but it is no longer the sole focus). Here is what that looks like:

First, we build a relatively small emergency fund. This could be somewhere between three and six months of expenses. Because emergency funds require a high degree of both liquidity and stability, the products of choice will be vehicles such as money market accounts, savings accounts, or penalty-free CDs. Here, our watchwords will be "safety, simplicity, liquidity." We don't want to overfund here as returns will be low and taxable. We can shoot for a reasonable amount of return, but not at the expense of liquidity.

Now we address the most important piece of any retirement plan: the income piece. Just like I know where to go for the piece of pizza that does the job every time, I look to other sources that produce income to build out this piece of the retirement strategy.

Social Security is, in essence, an annuity payout. A defined-benefit plan from your company is an annuity plan. If you hit the lottery and take the payout overtime? Yep, another annuity. The FedEx golf champion gets a $10 million lifetime annuity. When it comes to lifetime income, particularly for both spouses, an annuity is the product of choice. It is Sam's pizza and Curley's fries topped off with ice cold Birch Beer.

To give you an overview:

> *"An annuity is a contract between you and an insurance company in which you make a lump sum payment or series of payments and in return obtain regular disbursements beginning either immediately or at some point in the future. The goal of annuities is to provide a steady stream of income during retirement."*[4]

Annuities' guarantees are related to the ability of the issuing company to pay out their claims.

Which annuity combined with which growth products? This is where the science is. Because once we have matched up the budgetary needs with all fixed sources of income such as Social Security and pensions, and then funded the proper annuity to provide for any shortfall, the focus then shifts to growth. Then and only then. This is an important difference in our methodology and the results are greater predictability and potential peace of mind.

---

[4] Investopedia. "What is an annuity?"
https://www.investopedia.com/ask/answers/12/what-is-an-annuity.asp.

Curley's fries never disappoint.

This process, while inherently simple, must be followed in this sequence, if guarantees are important to you. The shift from growth first to income first is the strategy that puts predictability before performance. It ranks safety ahead of opportunity by moving into a retirement orientation with your retirement portfolio. It makes income "king" in your personal retirement plan.

You create your own income plan that can cover both spouses, thereby eliminating the number one concern facing retirees today, which is running out of money. Based on this model, our path forward is clear. We must lay a foundation of income using Social Security, any pension, and typically annuities to solidify a consistent and predictable paycheck. Once we have established our income, the balance of our retirement funds can go back to market-based assets aimed at beating inflation. Full throttle ahead. Now we are adding investments such as mutual funds, stocks, bonds, ETFs, and real estate to the recommendations. At Synergy, we work in concert with each individual client to structure their portfolio toward their expectation and comfort level, also known as risk tolerance.

Lastly, if important to you, we will turn the discussion to legacy planning and the proper products, or "tools" to facilitate that goal. For some, this is not important, while to others it is very much so. Case by case, we will craft your retirement plan to meet your exact specifications, goals, and dreams. You can take advantage of our team's combined seventy-plus years of experience and thousands upon thousands of planning meetings to simplify your process. Everyone is put on this earth and has God-given talents to do something. For myself and the rest of the advisors at Synergy, retirement planning is our talent, I think.

I would like to reinforce that, while we have complete conviction in the preceding process, we understand it is a different path than many other advisors choose for their clients. Another advisor might recommend a more "traditional" route of continuing to invest in mutual funds, or perhaps might suggest putting more bonds with a less volatile orientation into the portfolio. Yet, for those approaching retirement, projections are just that—educated guesses about what the market might do. At Synergy, we don't think this is a good way to establish your necessary income. If the market dips 10 percent tomorrow, your light bill won't somehow also be less. Based on a projection of market activity, what begins as a plan for you to get 4 percent of the account value for income each year may become 6 percent. Projections are not a guarantee and guarantees are what most of our clients desire.

So, we continue to use and advocate that market-based products be the products of choice to take aim at the effects of inflation and other life needs. While there are no promises of growth (or protections against loss of principal), market-based products have historically been used as a potential hedge against the impact of inflation. But we will always, always first build a guaranteed, predictable stream of lifetime, joint income before addressing growth needs. I believe that when searching out a retirement plan that will be a fit for you, the first thing you look for is a sense of trust with an advisor. Find that, and then trust that together you will craft the plan specifically designed to carry you through those thirty or forty years of retirement.

After all, income will always be "king" in the retirement planning process, and our decades of experience will hopefully lead you to the perfect retirement choices for your secure journey through what can be life's most exciting chapter. Enjoy it.

CHAPTER FIVE

One Island, Four Municipalities

One of the mysteries that I will never understand fully is how it makes any sense that a five mile stretch of sand has four governing bodies. With exception (and apologies) to Diamond Beach, which is just, in reality, an extension of Wildwood Crest, there are four distinct municipalities on this island called Wildwood. To the south is the Crest. To the west, West Wildwood. To the north, yep, North Wildwood. Smack dab in the middle is Wildwood itself. Each community has its own political hierarchy, maintaining its own mayor and councilmen and staff, police and EMT, as well as fire, and on and on and on. I will never truly be able to figure the economies of scale that go into that mix, but I do understand the virtual impossibility of joining them together. Each municipality has unique elements that they fight diligently to maintain, and fear that considering a change would dissolve their identities entirely.

Wildwood Divided

The Crest is lined with Oceanfront hotels staring out at the water. Our condo sits thirty feet away from where the Crest begins, as we are the last property in Wildwood. As such, we have made good friends over at Crest Community Church and enjoy the amazing apple fritters (and other treats) from Britton's bakery over on Pacific, as well. We frequently stop over at Harbor Light mini golf with the family and enjoy the challenges of eighteen miniature holes of golf in an evening of fun. As you move back into the mostly residential community, you find rows of houses built over the years, houses where dreams become reality and families flock for lifetimes of memories. And of course, no Crest experience can compete with going to Crest Tavern for the Wednesday-only chicken pot pie special.

Over on the West Wildwood side of town, the homes hug the bay. Grand structures impose the skyline along the water, boat slips teem with all types of ocean-worthy vessels in this small coastal refuge. I enjoy biking along the water and seeing the beauty of the marshes spreading out in a tranquil scene, quiet and peaceful.

Looking out at the ocean by the jetty in North Wildwood; one can never tire of the view

Moving to North Wildwood, you have the same oceanfront mega-properties, but now, as you move back onto the island, there are the tight-knit Irish and Italian communities. The North restaurants and bars stand ready to break out in an ethnic celebration any day of the week. Everything from bagpipes to Clydesdale teams of horses join the celebration—there's no need to wait for the weekend to celebrate life here.

Lastly, there is Wildwood proper. Here, the beach is lined with their famous Boardwalk and all the hustle and bustle associated with it. Moving onto the island, motels, condos, restaurants, and shops sprawl, with a hint of 1950s doo-wop culture lurking around every corner. The downtown section has struggled to recover the glory days of the 50s and 60s eras, but the faithful still flock to the boardwalk and all the thrills of a beach vacation.

Unfortunately, this diversity does not allow for the efficiencies a unified town would provide. Not one of them is willing to change or give up its uniqueness for lower taxes or being able to offer better services. All of them cling to their uniqueness and simultaneously strive to serve their constituents, some of whom live there year-round, and others just for the week of vacation (the dreaded Shoobies).

Financial Divides

When it comes to the financial community of advisors, the same sort of integration applies. For some, a *generalist* mentality is the drive. Generalists strive to serve their client base by appealing to clients of all ages to sustain their practice. They become adept at understanding market-based applications and predominantly using mutual funds. Let's call them Wildwood Crest. This group primarily aims for many of the desired results the market will bring: diversification, professional management, and flexibility, with literally thousands of funds to choose from. With so many options, and often more movement in and out of products, fee structures vary wildly. This variation often means a client will not fully understand the costs therein.

You see, each mutual fund has a prospectus, which must state the costs of the portfolio—the fees associated with owning the mutual fund shares and maintenance thereof. But there are numerous other fees not covered there. Internal transaction costs, and possible load costs (to name a few) are often something investors are unaware of. Check out the Securities and Exchange Commission's website discussing the fees of mutual funds to get an idea of how much of the proverbial fee iceberg is hiding under the surface.[5]

Often all of a client's accounts under management with a single broker will be "wrapped" together, called a wrap account. This allows the broker to better see what's happening comprehensively and allows consumers to just pay one overall fee. Sounds good, right? Well, the flip side is that when all fees are wrapped together, putting mutual fund fees, transactional fees, etc. all together and even adding the percentage point or two that a broker charges, this means that the client may not realize what they are paying for each investment or for management of those investments. It is critically important at all stages of life to know the costs of your investment plan, perhaps even more so in the retirement years, so you can effectively evaluate the efficiency of your plan.

So, for retirement planning, when mutual funds are used for income needs, they carry two considerable issues that, for me, cause concern: fees and volatility. Fees will, in some way or another, be present in all investment vehicles or services—whether this is a fee

[5] U.S. Securities and Exchange Commission. "Fast Answers: Mutual Fund Fees and Expenses."
https://www.sec.gov/fast-answers/answersmffeeshtm.html

for advice, a fee for professional management, or a fee to cover trading, developing, and marketing costs.

Obviously, the lower the fees the better, but fees are not inherently evil. If the advice and expertise they bring to the table are more valuable than the fees you pay for those services, then your money is well spent. However, if no service is provided and no support is given once the account is secured, then maybe not. Understanding and minimizing unnecessary fees is the key here. Also to the point is the market volatility involved in investing. The market can go up and the market can go down, and with it, your account values. The more up and down movement that happens in a small timeframe, the more volatility the market is said to have. Make no mistake, even mutual funds with more blue-chip stocks that are less "volatile" are still market-based investments that are subject to many risks. If someone is looking for guaranteed income, how can they plan for it from any non-guaranteed investment?

The right annuity for you will provide wave after wave of consistent monthly income.

Okay, let's go across the financial island to West Wildwood. Some retirement-focused professionals will only (and I mean only) recommend an annuity. I completely agree with them that, because in many cases, using the proper fixed indexed annuity with income riders (for more on this, please see the glossary section of the book) can be an integral part of an income strategy. That being said, an annuity is only one piece of the income puzzle. If annuities are the only products deemed necessary for retirement, then we ignore a retiree's need for growth and a legacy plan. If we stop with annuities, we come far short of a complete retirement plan.

Deciding what a retiree needs is determined on a case-by-case basis by conducting a detailed review of the client's income needs. This, coupled with a multitude of other pieces, will adequately address each person's unique retirement goals.

However, using the annuity (or any other product, for that matter) as one-size-fits-all is just wrong. Yes, income is "king" and needs to be established and guaranteed, but to ignore a retiree's need for growth to deal with inflation and increased medical costs is foolhardy. Let's give some consideration as to why a financial professional would do this. Why recommend an annuity only? Perhaps the representative's license is limited so as not to be able to develop other pieces of the desired comprehensive plan that a client needs put in place. If I were only licensed to sell insurance-related products, then an annuity would likely be my recommendation every time—as the saying goes, when all you have is a hammer, everything looks like a nail. But a solid platform for overall planning needs to go significantly beyond saying "annuities are the answer to every possible situation." I always counsel clients that when someone presents a one-size-fits-all strategy or takes products off the table without discussion, that perhaps they should seek a second opinion before acting.

Now to those in North Wildwood. Here we get to the group, pardon my insolence, that goes completely to the other side. The market in its multitude of choices is the only, and I repeat only, game in town here. Just like the ethnic pockets of Irish and Italian bastions deeply intrenched in the North end of the Island, change is not easy for them. Again, here I find reason for concern. Since I am completely aware of the strengths and weaknesses market-based products offer, I believe I understand which applications of these products might expose those strengths and weaknesses. That is why we do not recommend market-based solutions for income needs.

I believe a sense of arrogance is sometimes involved when a broker states unequivocally that his or her understanding of the market, coupled with the decades of experience their firm provides, will assure the couple walking through those retirement years financial success. Again, I define financial success in retirement as not running out of money in life and, regardless of experience, regardless of expertise, a purely market-based plan of investing in my opinion cannot provide that guarantee.

I do not question these folks' knowledge. I do not question their desire to provide for the client. I question using a financial tool, a strategy if you will, that is designed for pure growth when the need is clearly for income. In my opinion, the wrong tool for the job is being used. You don't use a saw to hammer in a nail and you don't use a product that's subject to the whims of the market to provide a guaranteed income.

I have seen all the nuances here. Reserve some cash for the hard times. So, how much cash is enough? And what is that piece of the portfolio earning? Is it worth the fees you are paying? After all, brokers earn money on the assets under their management regardless of performance.

Now we come into Wildwood proper. Here exists a mix of recreation and business, where shops and condos and homes and all exist side-by-side. Travel down Pacific Avenue and you will find old storefronts and shops from eras long gone: the doo-wop legacy. This bit of history is interspersed with new parks and renovated businesses trying to revitalize the downtown section. Move to the south and in just a few blocks you come upon the Boardwalk and the beach. It's a true mix of eclectic nostalgia and the vibrancy of the Boards.

At Synergy, our world of retirement strategies is much like the community of Wildwood. Build the income plan—a written, structured, predictable, annuity-based foundation for safety and security—and then move beyond to the growth world of investments. Combine the necessary fixed, predictable elements with the vitality and potential of growth elements in a mix designed to do one thing very well: retirement.

When we talk about assets aimed at beating inflation and potentially shoring up a legacy, we're talking about stocks, mutual funds, managed money accounts, bonds, real estate, collectibles, and any other viable choice that is in line with that client's goals and situations. Once built, we can support a plan with quality service that begins with the relationship between the advisor and the client and extends to our experienced support team to provide the service and support every client needs and deserves. It has taken over thirty years to craft this "financial Wildwood" and it has been refined and honed to a point that seems to work very well for our clients' needs.

Beyond that, at our firm we strive to cultivate a deeper relationship. We offer a host of ongoing social interactions, designed to parallel what our clients have told us they enjoy. Movie Day, Garden Day, golf events, and a Christmas party with more than a thousand attendees annually are just a few of those "social connections" unique to Synergy that build wonderful relationships with those who have trusted us for their retirement peace of mind. Perhaps the Wildwood approach we take at Synergy has combined the best of the four communities, after all.

So, which of the retirement communities will you choose to govern your Island? They are all available and are represented by the industry. I wholeheartedly believe in the planning strategies I use. That is not to say there are not cases to be made for going to a different part of the Island, but, for me, the risks are too high. Cindy and I have used this exact structure in our own retirement funding. Our strategy, when we retire, will establish an income using annuities combined with managed money for market growth, along with some fixed accounts. I have structured the plan to provide the income we need while preparing to aim for the growth we desire for future needs, as well.

I have in the past five to ten years seen a very strong movement by many more toward our philosophy. White papers from the Government Accountability Office, companies like Putnam, and investment analysts such as Ibbotson[6] now advocate more conservative planning and the inclusion of the fixed annuity into the income plan. Newer, stronger recommendations industry-wide advocate moving any "withdrawal rates" for income to below 3 percent distributions. This is in attempt to stretch those market-based funds through your lifetime. There are companies now recommending annuities who seemingly never knew how to spell the word before, all of which reinforces our strategies and methods. I understand that our conservative approach is just that, and for some it may not be their cup of tea. I get that. But for the thousands of clients who have trusted us, our part of the Island feels just right. Could you consider a visit to this island of predictability for your retirement needs, as well?

---

[6] Diana Britton. WealthManagement.com. March 7, 2018. "Ibbotson: Fixed Index Annuities Beat Out Bonds."
https://www.wealthmanagement.com/insurance/ibbotson-fixed-indexed-annuities-beat-out-bonds/
Government Accountability Office. March 2011. "Private Pensions: Some Key Features Lead to an Uneven Distribution of Benefits."
https://www.gao.gov/new.items/d11333.pdf

CHAPTER SIX

Using a Professional Property Manager

Having vacationed in Wildwood, and with a growing entourage making the trek for the annual beach vacation, the thought of buying our own place entered the conversation somewhere around 1997. In 1999, the condo we had rented for the past four seasons was on the market. Long story short, after doing the math and looking at some other options on the market as well, we were ready to buy. Again, I had done my research, but the final "test of the fleece," so to speak, rested on a whimsical possibility. That year, our moms had made the trip with us and I said to my wife, "If both your and my mom's maiden names are in the Wildwood phonebook, we will make our offer." Sure enough, there they were. Decision made. Offer presented and accepted. We were officially condo owners and had deepened our connection to the Island.

Knowing our inability to spend lengthy periods there and having an affinity for fall visits, we fully intended to use the property as an investment and rent it during those prime income rental weeks to offset our costs. To me, being willing to "share" the property meant we owned it, as opposed to it owning us. But being 347 miles away presented a host of details to handle. How would we secure tenants? Who would be there to provide access, clean the property weekly, and do the minor repairs that would inevitably arise? When someone pays to use your property, these and many other details must be in place. Enter the property manager.

We were fortunate to purchase a property in a large condo association and there was an onsite rental realtor in the building. Interestingly, as well, she originally hailed from the Pittsburgh area and was a perfect fit for our needs. For a reasonable percentage, she secures the clients, arranges the cleaning services, and has a team on site to handle minor needs as they arise. She also has a list of referrals available for major repair items, too, which is extremely helpful when needed. Thank you, Chris Henderson. For over twenty years, we have been blessed by this arrangement. Careful consideration went into building this plan and trusting others for help was a part of that plan.

A proper retirement planner will allow you to breathe easy about your future, and you can use your time to enjoy experiences, like performances at the Wildwood Convention Center!

I understand you are not reading this book for information about buying a condo. However, when building your future retirement needs and dreams, just as I had a need for an expert for my property needs, you will benefit by adding an ally to be your expert in retirement. Often, early in the conversation I have with folks who are considering using my services, I strive to have them really understand what I believe is of primary importance. I believe products are products and, for the most part, universally available. What they are seeking first is the relationship, the belief they can trust the advisor. Once that is secured, the rest will follow.

Finding Your Financial Professional

When you are finding the right guide for your finances in retirement, absolutely check an advisor out thoroughly. Licensure, history, references all need to be in place before considering any relationship with an advisor. What they specialize in, how they interact with their clients, what their support team looks like—these questions should all be asked and answered before moving forward in the relationship. For the most part, fairly early in the process, you get a feeling of whether this person is trustworthy, whether they are someone with whom you know you can have an ongoing working relationship. Find that and you are home. Once you have found a retirement specialist you feel is trustworthy, you are where you want to be.

Obviously, this person will have a responsibility to build the right plan for you using the proper tools to develop income and growth. Together, you will craft the specifics for your family's needs, but without the element of trust, you will get nowhere. If you don't get a healthy sense of trust, then, respectfully, I suggest you leave and search until you find it. We found an expert for our property needs. Now, your search must continue until you find the lifeguard your retirement plan needs, as well. After all, this relationship should be crafted with a long-term vision in mind, so take the time to do it right the first time.

Paying for Financial Guidance

Now, to the matter of costs. When it comes to the percentage our property manager charges, some might consider it to be expensive. Others on the Island charge less. However, in the case of our condo (as it does in most), the adage "you get what you pay for" holds true. I personally find our property manager's charge to be completely fair and in line with the level of service she provides.

Striving to control costs is human nature and wise. In my industry, financial professionals are paid in various manners, but they are all paid in one way or another. Those payments ultimately come from the client. Some are "fee only," meaning the advisor is not involved in placing or servicing the investment, just in providing paid advice to guide you to a product. Giving the idea of no bias, they are there to offer ongoing product choices and nothing more. Perhaps there is comfort in trusting this form of payment because the advisor will not be compensated beyond the cost of the recommendations. If there is a flaw here, in my opinion it is in the fact that, while critically important, product selection is only the tip of the process. The true value a relationship with an agent brings is provided year-by-year as they provide ongoing service, conduct annual reviews, and potentially help reduce emotional stress and its effects when the markets get bumpy. None of this relationship is developed when the only relationship is limited to product choices.

Some offer a management fee to use their expertise to develop an overall plan that includes ongoing service and management. Some offer annuities or bank products and are paid their commissions by the issuing company. Some, as we do, offer investments, bank products, and annuities, among other financial services.

When building a financial services retirement practice, you make a lifetime commitment to each client.

As I said earlier when talking about our "Wildwood" approach, at our firm, we use a variety of approaches combined. I personally am a Registered Representative of Global Financial Investment Services, LLC (GFIS), and clients pay me as a percentage of the securities GFIS manages. I am also one of several individuals on our staff that are licensed to sell insurance products through Synergy Group, Inc. These products include annuities, which we get paid for by the companies whose product we sell as a commission, which is built into the upfront cost of each product. Some of the other professional services available at the Synergy firm—outside of the services I offer—include fiduciary advisors (meaning advisors who are legally bound to act in your best interest) on staff as investment advisors representing Global Financial Private Capital. They are the ones who can charge a fee for putting together a plan, but most often they opt to get paid as a percentage of the assets they manage so that their pay is more closely tied with performance.

Regardless of who you work with and what kind of firm they are, you want to be sure you're working with a team that can provide comprehensive services, and at a cost you think is fair. Every percentage point you pay to someone that is beyond the value their product or service provides to you is a percentage point of your own money that isn't working for you.

So, just as I determined the fee my property manager charged was of more value to me than what it cost for those services, you must determine if a financial professional's costs are acceptable to you. We don't secure renters or cleaning services for our clients, but on a daily basis, we are there for them. In a firm devoted completely to serving the needs of retirees, for more than thirty years, we have been there for our clients. Our team of three advisors and twelve full-time professional staff serve the needs of our clients. Hundreds of calls are fielded weekly, covering a wide array of needs and are handled professionally, accurately, and promptly. Periodic face-to-face meetings with the client and our advisory team happen both on a scheduled basis (once or twice a year or quarterly) and on an as-needed basis. Our onsite CPA, Medicare associates, and insurance associates fill the need for expert advice to complement the financial planning needs of our clients, as well. Relationships with several of the area's foremost legal firms are in place as well, to round out our clients' needs for business continuity and estate planning needs.

When we drive out to the beach and look out we can see as far away as our eyes can manage. That's how your retirement plan should be too: completely visible, with no obstacles blocking your vision.

Just as with all decisions in life, whether purchasing a vacation/rental property or seeking a retirement advisor, good planning is called for. Seek out someone with whom you first sense a feeling of trust. Work together to craft *your* plan—not a cookie-cutter, off the shelf plan—and then reap the rewards those efforts will provide.

Yes, there will be costs. Yes, there will be some bumps. But when those bumps and waves do occur, both the client and the advisor will be prepared. Each must approach the process with open eyes, good communication, and some flexibility to hurdle every obstacle.

Seeing all the parts of your plan coordinated and working together can be a wonderful experience. It *should* be. We develop relationships in other areas of life with industry specialists and experts—many of us have our car guy, our computer guy, our handyman, and that guy who always knows the best way to get anywhere in town—and the same wisdom applies to this area of life, as well. The removal of these concerns for our clients is the reason we exist. Have you addressed these fundamental issues regarding your own accounts? If not, why?

CHAPTER SEVEN

Early Bird Specials

A s a younger man, I used to smile as I would see the senior crowd flock to the restaurants, seemingly only because they might save a few bucks. I think back to a Seinfeld episode where Jerry and his parents banter back and forth about this specific topic. When I first saw it, at the time I empathized so very much with Jerry and the fun he had at his folks' expense. The thought of eating so early and getting fewer options and smaller portions was easy to find humorous.

Now, at sixty-five, I am there. I eat less, so smaller portions are just fine. I like smaller crowds, so getting there before the rush works for my wife and me. Even a limited menu offers most of what I would choose anyway, so what's the big deal? Now I am falling asleep on the couch as the last of the restaurant's dinner crowd is being seated. Saving some money is just the icing on the cake. For the restaurants, they can extend the dinner hour and fill seats earlier, all the while increasing profits and hours of employment for their staffs. A different time of life yields a different perspective on the same issue.

These gulls know they will get the best breakfast if they arrive first. And if you plan ahead as much as these little guys, you'll have the best financial life possible in retirement.

Two areas of "early bird" retirement planning come into view for me here, as well, whether at the shore or at home. Pension elections and determining when to begin Social Security distributions—these two topics require numerous decisions that are worth seeking good counsel on and, when done properly, yield benefits over the remaining days of your life. Days that may very well number twenty to thirty years and, as such, it's important to get these decisions right. Let's look at both of these.

Pensions . . . an Endangered Bird

If you are fortunate enough to have a defined-benefit pension plan from your employment, good for you. Fewer and fewer of these plans are offered in today's environment. Public-sector employees and educators are the last bastions for these dinosaurs, and their providers are disappearing quickly. The reasons are obvious. It is extremely expensive to fund and guarantee the lifetime payments from these accounts. To deposit the funds required to provide twenty, thirty, or more years of pension payments requires an astonishing amount.

Employers have understandably flocked to defined-contribution plans (401(k), 403(b), and the like) to address the needs of their employees. How much easier is it to tell employees to place a portion of their salaries into the plan (and some employers still also contribute a certain percentage match) and then allow the employees to figure out how to make the plan provide the income. Quite often, folks feel inadequately prepared to make decisions on how to craft a plan that provides for those income needs and turn to an advisor for help.

But even for those who have a defined-benefit plan at work, decisions on when and how to take their earned benefits are often confusing. The "when" is obviously a combination of a variety of personal considerations. The "how" is often dictated by marital circumstances. Typically, an employee has at least two basic pension options. One is to take 100 percent of the benefits, knowing that when you die, that check will no longer come to your household. The other is to take a reduced paycheck for two lifetimes—that of you and your spouse. With this option, your monthly check will be lower, but it will keep coming to you or your spouse no matter who outlives whom. Deciding between these two options requires careful consideration. Some have a difficult time thinking it over, tempted by the allure of a higher check but put off by the idea that an early death might get the company off the hook on paying you. I see taking the full personal benefit with no spousal consideration to be, in most cases, unfair to the surviving spouse and probably unwise in the planning arena to do that, as well. Yet, for some, a detailed review of a life insurance policy combined with 100 percent no spousal protection option can be a viable option. This requires a detailed analysis of the individual situation, including the health considerations of both spouses. Obviously if both spouses have pensions and the budget needs are covered, then numerous options exist and need to be discussed in depth. A good retirement specialist can be invaluable in this area.

Social Security—A Good Egg or an Old Bird?

Now let's consider the question of when to start Social Security income. Let's start with some Social Security basics.[7] In normal circumstances, if you are qualified (you qualify after having worked forty quarters) you can begin payments from Social Security anywhere between the ages of sixty-two and seventy. There are a few basic rules critical to deciding when this will provide maximum benefits for your unique situation. First off, you might consider whether you have reached "full retirement age" (FRA). This is the age when, regardless of any other income, Social Security will be paid without any portion being reduced by that income.[8]

---

[7] Myself, Synergy Group and G.F. Investment Services ("GFIS") do not provide tax, accounting or legal advice. Any tax, accounting or legal concepts discussed are not intended to provide specific tax, accounting or legal advice or serve as the basis for any financial decisions. Individuals are advised to consult with their own accountant and/or attorney regarding all tax, accounting and legal matters. Synergy Goup or and GFIS are not affiliated with the Social Security Administration or any governmental agency.]

[8] Social Security Administration. 2019. "Full Retirement Age."
https://www.ssa.gov/planners/retire/retirechart.html

Your Full Retirement Age	
Year of Birth	**Full Retirement Age**
1937 or earlier	65
1938	65 and 2 months
1939	65 and 4 months
1940	65 and 6 months
1941	65 and 8 months
1942	65 and 10 months
1943—1954	66
1955	66 and 2 months
1956	66 and 4 months
1957	66 and 6 months
1958	66 and 8 months
1959	66 and 10 months
1960 or later	67

For those born between 1943 and 1954, that age is sixty-six. Younger than that, your "FRA" will be increased year-by-year as detailed by Social Security. So, if you retire at sixty-two and have no income from employment, you can collect your Social Security benefit. If you are still working at sixty-two but considering taking your Social Security, there is a whole host of tax implications to consider, which the Social Security Administration outlines on its website: www.ssa.gov. The tax implications of earning a paycheck and collecting Social Security simultaneously disappear in the month you reach your full retirement age—you can keep the income from both your Social Security check and paycheck. As I said, though, prior to full retirement age, there are restrictions on how much you can earn from a job while receiving a Social Security check, so be careful to enlist the help of a good planner to be prepared for this.[9]

So, if the coordination of your employment and the determination of when to start collecting Social Security is well in hand, the next step is where recommendations vary widely from advisor to advisor. Social Security payout amounts are reduced 8 percent per year from your full retirement (for those born 1943-1954—those younger will have a slightly different affectation) for each year before that date. So, retiring at sixty-two will reduce your payments by 25 percent, but you'll have forty-eight more months of benefits than waiting to full retirement age. Wait until age seventy, and payouts go up 8 percent for each year you waited, but keep in mind that the Social Security Administration won't provide you a check if you were planning to wait until seventy but predeceased your birthday. These same payout percentage considerations apply to your spouse if they are filing a spousal claim based off your work history, which is something worth considering closely. [10]

Many advisors recommend (as does the Social Security Administration and the Government Accountability Office) to wait as long as possible to begin payments so as to maximize those monthly amounts. Without a doubt, the longer one waits, the bigger the

---

[9] Social Security Administration. 2019. "Getting Benefits While Working." https://www.ssa.gov/planners/retire/whileworking.html

[10] Social Security Administration. 2019. "If you were born between 1943 and 1954 your full retirement age is 66." https://www.ssa.gov/planners/retire/1943-delay.html

checks will be—providing you live long enough to receive them. Regardless, the vast majority of Social Security recipients have begun receiving checks by age sixty-six. There are a variety of reasons for making that decision. I have experienced the loss of family, friends, and clients who never got a dime because they elected to wait and simply did not live long enough to collect, and I also know those who are able to collect much more because they waited.[11]

I have heard much "conventional wisdom" on the subject, and many in the personal finance field advocate waiting as long as possible, ideally to age seventy, to begin withdrawing benefits so you get the highest monthly check. However, what if you don't live long enough to reach seventy, or to whenever it was that you were postponing benefits? Then Social Security pays you nothing. Say you do make it to age seventy, though, you will be deep into your retirement years before Social Security has paid you more in total than it would have had you started benefits early, and that is providing they are still paying full benefits down the road as well.

What if, at the end of your working years or after reaching full retirement age, even if you don't need the income, you begin to collect and invest the after-tax benefits? Wouldn't those funds potentially produce some rate of return? Would your invested money not be available to increase your retirement income when combined with your continuing Social Security payments down the road? Then you'd have the money in your pocket, figuratively speaking, regardless of when God brought you home? For many, this might be a good decision despite conventional wisdom.

Without knowing your situation and goals, it's hard to say what each individual should or shouldn't do. So, the real bottom line of

---

[11] Matthew Frankel. The Motley Fool. April 2, 2017. "Why Do So Many People Claim Social Security at 62?"
https://www.fool.com/retirement/2017/04/02/why-do-so-many-people-claim-social-security-at-62.aspx

the discussion on Social Security really is this: As important of a decision as this is, I would hope that you seek good counsel on this decision because, once elected, you will live with your decision for the balance of your and your spouse's lives.[12]

The fact is, unless you can provide an exact date of when you will die, it is impossible to know the "ultimate best choice" to implement income from your Social Security. I usually joke and ask people to check on the bottom of their left heel for an expiration date. Obviously, no such date exists. Having a good conversation with your retirement advisor that includes your Social Security decision—particularly how it will relate to your other assets, as well— is not only wise but a critical part of crafting your income plan. You will also need to consider your health and the family histories of you and your spouse.

---

[12] Neither Synergy Group or GFIS provide tax, accounting or legal advice. Any tax, accounting or legal concepts discussed are not intended to provide specific tax, accounting or legal advice or serve as the basis for any financial decisions. Individuals are advised to consult with their own accountant and/or attorney regarding all tax, accounting and legal matters. Our firm is not affiliated with the Social Security Administration or any governmental agency.

A skilled fisherman will know where to cast the line. Although he might not guarantee a decent catch, he can make the wisest guess nonetheless. Same with Social Security: with an experienced professional, you'll be able to cast the line for the best catch possible.

Your advisor should help you develop an income plan and provide the summary to you in writing. Has your advisor provided you with a written, predictable plan? If not, you should request one. It should be harmonious with your budget and address the potential effects of inflation on that budget, too. Remember, "income is king" in retirement, so good income planning results in a smoother, more predictable sail through those golden years. Consider the value of planning as early as possible to potentially provide yourself savings and benefits in as many areas as possible. Do your "early bird special" preparation as young as possible. If you sense the need for help, let me know.

CHAPTER EIGHT

Fall Migration

O ne of the most amazing times at the shore is the fall. Some-
time toward late September, flocks of birds begin their
southward journey. The V formations of the flying geese
cut through the sky. Wave after wave of squawking waterfowl
winging their way to warmer climates.

But then a few weeks later, October happens, and the real magic
begins (at least as far as Cindy and I are concerned). Starting ever
so subtly, the monarch butterflies begin to appear. First, it's just one
every few hours. Sometimes pushed madly along by the ocean
breezes, they make their way south, one vegetation-covered sand
dune at a time. Day by day, the numbers build until every few
minutes another beautiful, fragile-winged creature floats by on the
long journey to Central America. Caught up in the corner of our
condo's ten-story structure, they must dance upward until they
reach the rooftop to clear the property—coincidentally, their path
takes them right in front of our balcony. Let the show begin.

They carry no GPS except the one God built into them, but these
fragile beauties of nature will continue undaunted until they reach
their ancestral home. Innately infused with instincts learned from
the generations that came before them, the process provides a system of life preservation and regeneration that ensures future wings
of golden beauty will ride along the shore breezes for the

foreseeable future. Once completed, the process will begin all over again in reverse order, and on and on it goes.

Retirement gives thought to not only our future needs. For many, retirement also brings the fourth financial component into the discussion: legacy planning.

To review, there are four different and distinct areas of financial need for all retirees. Liquidity is for emergencies. This might call for products (preferably ones with guarantees) that provide income for daily expenses, and investments aim to potentially provide for future needs.

Each distinct area needs a plan and requires funds to be placed into proper product choices based on the needs of the client. For some, the discussion now shifts to the final piece of the puzzle. Legacy planning. Legacy planning is synonymous with migrating funds from one generation to the next through planning and patterning for the transfer of wealth.

Planning for a Legacy

This final piece is not universally a part of everyone's plan. Some have no children, so the focus beyond both spouses' income or preservation does not exist. Perhaps philanthropical people wish to open the discussion to what charities may be in their hearts, or they may consider favorite family members as their heirs. But, in my experience, legacy planning when children are not part of the discussion is vastly different.

Sometimes even when a person or couple has children, I hear something to the effect of "What we have is left for only us. We love our kids, but we kept them healthy, well clothed, and fed. We provided for their educations and now that they are on their own, what is left is going to take care of us. Certainly, if anything beyond that is left, those funds are headed to the kids. We love them to death, but the legacy plan is not the prime consideration."

Because they have already provided way beyond basic needs and have given to the kids over the course of time, they consider that mission completed. Now their focus is back to the two of them, just as it was in the beginning when they made that lifetime commitment, all those long years ago. Generally speaking, many couples echo something to the effect of "The kids are doing fine and they have told us to use what we have for us." There's nothing selfish here; it's just a decision to now focus on the job at hand, which is a financially successful retirement.

For those desiring to discuss legacy issues, the conversation shifts to different strategies, different products, different priorities. We'll prioritize things like the simplicity of a transfer, how to reduce taxes, and how to leverage what is available. The financial tools we use for income and growth are different here and require unique strategies and structure. We'll consider how to address any extenuating circumstances that may exist.

Now, don't get me wrong—although we often work in conjunction with estate planning attorneys and tax professionals to help our clients with their legacy plans, we at Synergy are not estate planning attorneys. We don't give legal advice, and we can't establish a trust or write a will. Yet, it's undeniable that there is a significant upside to planning ahead when it comes to leaving a legacy. As I said, certain products may be easier or more efficient to pass across generations than others. And that's where we come in.

When it comes to any tricky situations you have in your family, you may need to honestly ask yourself, would an inheritance negatively affect a beneficiary's income if they have a disability? Does a beneficiary have the capacity to handle large sums of money, or does thought need to be given to a drug or alcohol problem? Do you want to ensure the funds to stay in the family in case the in-laws become the out-laws?

Some families work a lifetime to build their estate only to see the next generation wipe it out in a matter of years or months with frivolous spending. Ouch! So, what to do? An estate planning attorney can help you create legal documents such as wills or various kinds of trusts. Trusts can systematically disperse funds over time to perhaps allow your beneficiaries time to mature and consider thoughtful use of their inheritance. Certain financial products can be set to distribute out over a period of time so as to reduce beneficiaries' potential temptation to spend it all so quickly. Now is the time, while you have the opportunity to have these conversations with your family, to lovingly share your desires (not your commands). Use the time you have to build the relationships that can give you trust that wisdom will prevail after you have passed on.

Taxes, Legacy, and Your IRA

Perhaps it would be appropriate to discuss an example of an opportunity for legacy planning and how working with a financial professional can help you cover all your bases. As we have already mentioned, at age seventy-and-one-half, you will be required to begin distributions from your 401(k) or IRA. Remember, you have never paid taxes on money in your qualified retirement accounts. But they are tax-deferred, not tax free. The government requires you to begin taking a certain percentage of your saved qualified accounts based on your age and life expectancy. Otherwise, you face a 50 percent tax of what you should have taken. As I said, seventy-and-one-half is the age at which you must begin to take that required percentage; the often-dreaded Required Minimum Distributions (RMD). Dreaded, because it means paying taxes on funds that have never been taxed and which you may not necessarily need in your budget yet. If that is the case, you now have a decision to make: What do you do with these funds? You can spend these funds, which could be a good choice. You can give them away, another good choice, which I have heard described as "giving with warm hands instead of cold." You can reinvest them, which also may be a good choice but, if you wish to do so, I always ask, why? What future need for these funds do you anticipate? But perhaps there is another good choice you may overlook.

If the decision is to reinvest your required minimum distribution, usually those funds ultimately will pass to the children. But, is there a better way to do that?

It warrants an in-depth conversation with your financial professional about your goals, health, income, etc. For instance, I've had clients in good health who are legacy-minded who decided that some kind of permanent life insurance was the best approach. In that case, they paid their RMDs into the life insurance policy, building up funds that would eventually be passed to their beneficiaries, tax free. Some policies allow you to borrow against the balance, meaning you can still access a portion of the money you have paid in if your income situation changes (although it will in turn decrease the amount that is paid to your beneficiaries).[13]

Another possibility is to donate the balance or a significant portion of your IRA or 401(k) to your church, school, or favorite charity. This is done by using what is called a Charitable Remainder Trust. In this scenario, the asset owner continues to draw income from the assets but, on death, the "remainder" left in the trust will go to the charity designated as the beneficiary. This can be an effective way to ensure your favorite cause is funded after you're gone, while also significantly reducing the taxes your estate faces both now and in the future.[14]

Again, any strategy or product you use is going to depend greatly on your personal circumstances and goals, but I can give you an idea of what *can* be done. Hopefully you may understand the importance

---

[13] The Balance. 2019. "Estate Planning Basics."
https://www.thebalance.com/estate-planning-4073957

[14] Fidelity Charitable. "Charitable Remainder Trusts."
https://www.fidelitycharitable.org/philanthropy/charitable-remainder-trusts.shtml]

of working with a financial professional who can think outside the box. Building a financial strategy that keeps taxes and legacy plans in mind includes taking into account more than just basic market growth projections.

The many exciting rides at the Wildwood Boardwalk can be yet another reminder of how volatile life—and retirement—can be.

Going back to where I began this chapter—monarch migration is the pinnacle of the wonder found in nature. The multitude of butterfly wings that swoop past our balcony is not just impressive because of the express beauty of the delicate insects, but also because it is representative of the monarch's entire life transfer process. They migrate on their way to mate, beget eggs, and begin the next generation who will traverse the same path. I find beauty, too, in a well-planned and executed transfer of wealth that occurs with good, thoughtful planning. Planning requires knowledge, and knowledge is something a good retirement planner should bring to the table.

So, assuming legacy planning is important to you, there are two basic choices embodied in the preceding examples. Option one gives money to your family and the IRS. Option two gives money to your family and your favorite charity. You get to decide. Of course, you could simply give the after-tax IRA balance and the insurance funds to the kids as well, if that was your intention. Perhaps you simply need someone to help you understand what your options are, and how each will play into your goals and dreams.

CHAPTER NINE

Sand Dunes and Sand Pipers

G od knows what He is doing. In areas along the coast, natural barriers (and manmade copies) line the shore to protect the beaches from tidal surges when the weather turns bad. These "dunes" are filled with grasses and shrubs whose root systems protect the sand from eroding from the effects of wind and water. Teeming with life, they provide relief from the flatness of the beach by adding a sprinkling of color and serving as a refuge for wildlife. Birds such as sand pipers nest there. Butterflies feed and shelter in the bushes and shrubs, and the sand is teeming with everything from crabs to the occasional rabbit or two.

Scattered among the plant-life, even crops are present such as beach plum shrubs that yield what will later be and jams and jellies for the breakfast table. But the true reason dunes exist are for protection. To be there as a buffer to the surging storm. To protect property and lives by doing whatever is possible when the weather becomes impossible, and it will.

In retirement, "dunes" are created for the specific needs of the more mature generation for their protection, as well. Let's look at a few. I counsel always on the wisdom of good legal planning documents. Obviously in this area, the expertise of a sharp legal mind is necessary. We work very closely with numerous law firms we have come to know over the years and who our clients can trust for their knowledge, integrity, and fairness. By working with several, we can serve the geographical needs of our client base and refer them to firms with different levels of focus. Typically, in my opinion, a comprehensive package might include a will, health care and financial powers of attorney documents, and a living will. In my observations, these are adequate when combined with proper beneficiary listings. For most, this is sufficient and cost effective. For others, more detailed documents such as specific types of trusts may be the attorney's recommendation, but the network of affiliates we have created are poised to handle whatever need washes ashore.

We recently began a program called an ICE Key (In Case of Emergency), which is a computer thumb drive containing a listing of your physician's information, your medications, and a copy of your power of attorney for health care purposes. We encourage our clients to keep this on their keychains, readily available when needed for an emergency. It keeps the information and the documents detailing who has the authority to act if you are incapacitated on site and accessible. We have begun this program to provide, at our cost, this potentially life-saving tool to our clients. I firmly believe it will be instrumental in saving lives over the upcoming years because the necessary information will be readily available. When introduced to this tool, it seemed a natural fit for us to offer it to our clients.

As a firm specializing in the retirement community, it's the small differences multiplied over and over again that I believe make Synergy such an asset to those we serve. This is effectively another protective "dune" our firm offers in part because of our special focus on retirement planning.

I mentioned sand pipers at the beginning of this chapter, so let's consider how they might fit in. What unique, wonderful little fellows these guys are. If you have ever been to the beach, I'm sure you have smiled as you watched the antics of these miniature, cartoon-like creatures. Usually, you will find them one hundred, two hundred, or more, dancing a mad dash with the waves. As if one, they in unison dart in and out with each wave, frantically searching the sand for tiny tidbits of food, all the while making it appear that if so much as a drop of water touched them, they would melt away into the surf. These tiny little guys find safety and security in their masses. It is as if, because there are so many of them, they offer protection to one another. Safety in numbers, if you will, makes the sand pipers feel secure.

I am going to use that concept of "safety in numbers" to expound on my next point. As a firm dealing exclusively with seniors, a discussion on long-term care is a part of the planning process, too. We believe there are several viable solutions here, and that a thorough review of your options is wise to determine the best strategy for you. Oftentimes, the discussion will include long-term care insurance. Here is where hundreds upon hundreds, thousands upon thousands of individuals combine their premium dollars to protect one another. Here is where, because we stand together, we minimize the individual risk. This won't protect anyone from needing care, but from being potentially financially ruined if you do require help. It is not the correct choice for all, but it is wise for all to investigate. Here is where we in unison dart in and out with each wave.

I can speak to the numbers of how many will need care and the insane costs involved, whatever the level of care they need. I can discuss the tax advantages provided by owning this coverage, and the assets Pennsylvania law will shield if coverage is in place. Just like each individual sand piper, you must act to be protected. I have witnessed firsthand the results of both good and poor planning. This is why we discuss this in our planning sessions and why we have in-house insurance professionals on our team for these very issues. We have other professionals available, too, to discuss Medicare and taxes, such as our in-house CPA.

In life and in retirement, storms will come. What preparation we make, what affiliations we put in place, and who we trust all will be a part of how our safety net is constructed. Long-term care in-surance certainly is not needed or correct for everyone, but for some it does an amazing job. Good retirement planning includes becoming aware of all the options for covering the costs of nursing home and home health care, if needed. This part of the plan should be addressed by all those walking through this stage of life. Often, advisory firms who do not specialize in retirement may not be equipped to do so. It's important that whoever is helping you has strong connections with legal firms who focus on senior clientele and their specific needs. We do.

As you can see, the line for a pastry at Britton's Gourmet Bakery is out the door. If I had planned more, I might have already been eating the apple fritter I was craving that morning.

CHAPTER TEN

Beach Erosion: The Effects of Wind and Rain

Having spent ten to twelve weeks a year since 1999 at Wildwood, I tell folks we have lived somewhere around four years in New Jersey over the past twenty years. While we are still considered non-local (semi-Shoobies) by those who live there, we still have experienced much of what the changing seasons bring to the area, including the beach. Wildwood, as with most ocean communities, has the benefits of the frequent ocean breezes (so much so that we have nicknamed it Wildwind). In the spring, those breezes act like an enormous air conditioner and draw wonderful, cooling air as it passes over the water (just beginning to warm from winter). It brings that cool stream of air to our doors and balconies and provides a God-ignited cooling system late into June. Just the opposite occurs in the fall. Late into October as the water retains its summer warmth, the breeze now moderates the fall temperatures. The winds create an extended time of the wonderfully comfortable, moderate temperatures of fall, allowing them to prevail a bit longer.

When the winds rage, occasionally they push the water across the open sand. Sometimes external influences affect our investments, as well. Are you prepared for these financial storms?

The effects of those winds can be detrimental, too. The effects of erosion caused by these winds require continuous efforts to maintain the beauty and usability of that wonderful beach. Patio furniture and doors and windows are continuously dusted with the residue carried on the wind and need frequent attention to look good. When the winds are strong and come from the land into the ocean as the waves crest, tall plumes of mist blow back from them into the sea. You get a very tactile sense of just how powerful erosion actually is when you walk along the water's edge on a windy morning. As the sand pelts against your skin, it feels like a sand blaster aimed at your legs.

Erosion: Overpaying Taxes

Just as with the wind, the inescapable effects of erosion in our retirement portfolios comes from the equally powerful force of taxation. When crafting a retirement plan, obviously the reduction of spendable income to reflect the eroding dollars remaining after taxes are paid must be considered. A budget requires useable dollars to fund it, and when those dollars head out to Harrisburg or Washington, they no longer are in the checking account. That is one reason Synergy houses a CPA in the office to analyze each opportunity to reduce the effects of that erosion.

The job of the CPA is to be certain to do proper tax planning and reporting. The job of the advisor is to bring products into play to reduce or mitigate those taxes with advance preparation. Here is where we might have a discussion of possibly funding a Roth account while a person is still employed or, if retired, discuss systematically converting 401(k) or traditional IRA accounts to a Roth option. Here we might also discuss taxation on Social Security benefits and the possibility of determining investment allocations that might give us the opportunity to reduce that tax bill. Here we might also discuss strategies for gifting in ways that benefit our abilities to itemize an income tax form and realize greater tax benefits when filing our tax return.

To paraphrase a quote from Supreme Court Justice Learned Hand, no one is expected to pay more taxes than required—we are all able to structure our accounts to pay the least amount of tax legally possible. While we are not tax or legal professionals, we have relationships with tax and legal professionals with whom we coordinate these plans in order to control that tax erosion. Our clients are able to draw from a collective experience and knowledge in this area that provides not only an understanding of the tax code, but, equally important, a knowledge of products that can be useful in erosion control. Having a good, open discussion on tax considerations and combining the advisors' experiences with our CPA's knowledge makes for powerfully efficient planning. We collaborate to minimize the eroding effects of taxation on the client's accounts, resulting in more spendable income.

Erosion: The Effects of Inflation

One other significant contributor of beach erosion comes from the effects of water. Insidiously, wave by wave, tidal flow by tidal flow, the sands are carried from north to south. The winter months with stronger tidal effects often leave gullies, needing massive equipment to reshape and smooth out the beach topography when spring arrives. This is a less obvious erosion because its results are more difficult to see. However, step into the surf and, as you walk out into the waves you will feel the undulating sand bars hiding beneath those waters. As you move forward, the water deepens to a point. Then, you climb up the sand bar and what was waist deep water is now ankle deep. The continuous migration of the sand is hard to see, but you become keenly aware of it as you immerse yourself in the water. Equally of importance are the effects these underwater patterns may cause, contributing to a riptide effect. This is again unseen, but riptides are the cause of many a scare if not a downright tragedy.

This sometimes hidden (but nonetheless powerful) effect of erosion on our portfolios can be seen in the often overlooked and underestimated results that time and inflation bring to bear. In today's America, retirement can be twenty, thirty, or more years. Invariably this period of inflation will occur and invariably spending power will decrease. If inflation averages 3 percent and you live twenty years to enjoy your retirement, the purchasing power of $5,000 today will only provide $2,719 then. Said another way, it will require $9,030 twenty years from now to purchase what $5,000 does today. Extend those retirement years out to be thirty years and you will need $12,136 to purchase that same $5,000-worth of goods and services.

Obviously, the exact future timeline and percentage of inflation isn't something we can know. But the income-reducing erosion of funds lurking beneath the waters is powerful and must be brought into the discussion. At Synergy, as previously discussed, we build progressively (liquidity-income-growth-legacy) and this is often part of the discussion with clients of our need for potential future growth. Here, by choosing market-based investments, we will craft the elements necessary to prepare for future income needs. Of course, these assets will be subject to loss due to market risk, which is why we don't want to be dipping into them month after month for income. But with years to wait for drops and recoveries, there isn't a better mechanism than the market for beating inflation. Here we will install a plan to be prepared for what lies beneath the water, unforeseen but still powerful. The options are as wide as the ocean in front of me when I am in Wildwood.

We want our clients to feel as excited and carefree as this monster truck. In retirement you shouldn't worry about driving within the lines. Instead, we want you to be adventurous and go over those jumps!

Working with the client, we will structure an investment plan unique to their preferences, situation, and goals. Bonds, stocks, real estate, ETFs, or mutual funds are all available and all on the table for the discussion. By understanding their risk comfort and how these assets will interplay with the rest of their finances and goals, we are guided to the recommendations we will offer. By having already built the income plan, the doors are flung wide open to now structure a plan where we can take on more. This includes market risk in a tradeoff for the potential to deal with what the unstoppable reality of inflation will bring in the future. The beach is a beautiful place, but to keep it that way requires work and planning. Putting in the work and planning with a firm focused on retirement will go a long way toward crafting a retirement prepared to handle the erosion caused by inflation.

CHAPTER ELEVEN

Lighthouses, Seagulls, and Ocean Tides

Traveling along the coast of the New Jersey shore line, you'll see various communities have constructed lighthouses to provide guidance for the seafaring fisherman and travelers of the world. Perhaps in today's modern world with GPS and radar tracking making it easier for them to navigate, lighthouses are less important. However, I do believe these lighthouses continue to provide a sense of comfort and assurance for those looking in from the ocean. It serves as a good old-fashioned guiding light streaming out to meet them.

I believe, I would hope, that at Synergy we provide a lighthouse, or a beacon, if you will, of knowledge and stability for our clients. The current generation of retirees are becoming much more comfortable with the electronic connections the world offers today, however, they still find peace and security in the relationships with a personal advisor on whom they depend, especially when the financial world surrounding them becomes foggy.

One thing of which you can be certain, if you're at the beach, you will see a bunch of seagulls. Amazing creatures. They flow effortlessly on the air currents, constantly moving up and down the beach in search of food. Sometimes they're diving in the water for fish or cracking a clamshell on the pavement (they have amazing adaptability). At other times, they silently swoop down to grab a French fry or a piece of pizza from an unwary vacationer's hand. These guys eat constantly; birds after my own heart.

I think the retirement lesson that seagulls demonstrate to me is the need to be prepared and to continually monitor our retirement programs. The program that you built initially with your advisor will need to be monitored and changed as your circumstances do. Sometimes, a life-changing event warrants a revisit of your strategy. Other times, it's a change in tax laws or other investment rules that will affect the plan. Ongoing regular meetings with your advisor are vital to a successful retirement plan. Just like seagulls demonstrate a high degree of flexibility and adaptability (and sometimes leave an undesired souvenir on an unlucky traveler), you need to be ready to stay ahead of financial changes that will occur.

The owner of this GTO has taken care of it for years, and it's still in pristine condition. Your retirement deserves the same attention and care.

Lastly, I'd look to the movement of the water. The tides, if anything, are predictable. You can set your clock to the incoming and outflowing tides. If the paper says high tide will be at 11:53, it will be exactly 11:53. The consistency of the effect the lunar pull has on our oceans, these huge bodies of water, is hard to comprehend. Yet, there it is. The effects this twice-daily dance of the water can make for a source of daily amazement. When coupled with other forces of nature, the water can go from a predictable tide to a dangerous situation, and can do so quite rapidly.

Likewise, in retirement the investment world will have its daily ebb and flow. Although past performance is not indicative of future results, we do see patterns in investing. There's usually a market bump after the midterms.[15]

Federal regulations or news about government shutdowns often sets of a bit of wobbling volatility.[16] These fairly predictable outcomes to me are like the tides, reflecting the constant changes, the myriad of influences affecting the normal market rhythm. However, it is when those outside forces burst onto the scene that the game changes and often quickly and dramatically. When Greece declares bankruptcy, or the U.K. decides to "Brexit." When an under-regulated industry has a bubble burst. That is when the relationship with a good advisor will benefit the most. Someone who can help calm the emotional waters when necessary can be greatly beneficial at these times. Remember we teach that market-based investments are aimed at growth for the long term, for future needs. But that doesn't mean they won't meet plenty of short-term volatility that

---

[15] Jeff Sommer. New York Times. November 2, 2018. "The Stock Market Typically Rises After the Midterm Elections. This Year Is Anything But Typical." https://www.nytimes.com/2018/11/02/business/stock-market-rises-midterm-elections.html

[16] Fidelity. December 21, 2018. "What Shutdowns Can Mean for Investors." www.fidelity.com/viewpoints/market-and-economic-insights/government-shutdown-impacts-markets-investors

could result in losses of their principal and earnings. Based on my observations, market ebbs and flows are a bit easier to weather for the long term when your next month's income is not involved. Knowing you are working with someone you can trust is important to instill confidence in the plan even when the surges in the market push the financial tides into areas of discomfort.

CHAPTER 12

Sunset Beach

J ust a fifteen-minute ride south of Wildwood down to Cape
May, there is an area where you run out of New Jersey and
nothing but ocean remains. It is called Sunset Beach. What a
beautiful way for a state to end. A quaint little niche where the sun
sinks into the western sky in some of the most vibrant shades of
color on God's paint pallette. Adding to this special moment, with
each setting sun, taps echo from a bugle as a veteran's flag is lowered
from the top of the flagpole and retired forever. It's hard to find a
more patriotic, beautiful way to close a day.

A black and white photo can't begin to do justice to a beach sunset.

In the movie "Six Days, Seven Nights," Harrison Ford says to Anne Heche a line that goes something like, "This is an island, Babe, and if you didn't bring, it ain't here." Life is very much like that. The things we bring to life makes our life (our island) what it is. The person we become comprises all those things we bring onto the island we are. The choices we make or don't, that is our Wildwood. It is sometimes hard to think of Wildwood as an island. But, if you don't cross one of those three bridges from the mainland, you need a boat to get here. It is sometimes hard to see how the decisions we make in life craft our island, but every bridge we cross, every lesson we learn in life, makes us who we are. Building on the traits and traditions of our past, we reshape our island continuously as we walk each day through our lives. It's in the people we draw near to. For me, my life would have looked so much different were it not for shaping of my island by the amazing woman God brought into my life. Thank you, Cindy.

The places we work in, live in, choose to worship God in, all build us piece by piece into the island we become until the day we hopefully stand before our Creator and hear the words, "Well done, my good and faithful servant." We end our weekly radio show with the thought, "do the best planning you possibly can and remember, God will provide."

In retirement, we craft an island, as well. We invest for years to build the necessary funds that we believe will carry us through those golden years. We choose a financial strategy to deal with the necessities of today, all the while giving thoughtful consideration to the needs of the future and perhaps even beyond our own future. We at Synergy have crafted—plan by plan, need by need—what we believe is a unique methodology designed to help our clients navigate a more predictable path to and through their retirement years.

Those who are wise in the years before retirement (I call it pretirement) give thought to what is necessary to achieve their desires in a fashion comfortable for them. They take the time to understand the difference between building a retirement account and living off the proceeds of one. They give thought to what will fill the void when the days do not consist of eight to ten hours of work and, regardless of what they choose to fill that void, they design their plan based on how that will look.

This is the first thing you'll see when you visit our firm. I hope it'll be the beginning of a new, exciting adventure for you.

They come to understand that, similar to a resort island, many things cost more than we anticipated, and our plan to bring all we need to our retirement island may benefit from good alliances. A good retirement-oriented advisor is such an alliance. Seek one out and find someone you can truly trust. Together, you will bring the necessary pieces onto your island to provide for the wants, needs, and desires your retirement requires and deserves. You will also prepare for the storms that invariably will come. Regardless of whether you are preparing for or walking through retirement, good planning is vital.

I am blessed to have as much as possible an understanding of where this retirement practice flows in the future. I have a son who quite honestly has moved this firm lightyears forward with his heartfelt dedication to this agency, all while maintaining our desired relational style of interaction with our clients and other allies. I have other family members who, on a daily basis serve our clients in so many ways. And of course, I have the possibility, the hope, that Synergy's future will continue for generations to come, as some of my eight grandkids may perhaps make their way into the firm.

God places everyone on this earth for some unique reason. I have been and continue to be blessed to serve others by crafting their retirement plans. I help them establish, as much as possible, the islands of their dreams. It gives me joy to see the results of successful planning in the stories my clients share as we meet to maintain the plans we have in place. To see our staff, the amazing support team we have been so blessed with, handling all the service needs that arise each day and fulfilling the promises made to provide great service. It amazes me how this has all grown: straight from such humble beginnings in the basement of our home. I understand that we have, for whatever reason, been blessed by God, and all credit for any of that begins and ends there.

Thank you, Lord.

Glossary of Terms

401(k)

A traditional 401(k) is an employer-sponsored plan that gives employees a choice of investment options. Employee contributions to a 401(k) plan and any earnings from the investments are tax-deferred. You pay the taxes on contributions and earnings when the savings are withdrawn. As a benefit to employees, some employers will match a portion of an employee's 401(k) contributions. Income taxes on matching funds also are deferred until savings are withdrawn.[17]

These plans have nonprofit and government employee counterparts in the 403(b), 457, and Thrift-Savings Plans, as well as after-tax Roth options.

401(k), 403(b), and TSA

These are various plans available, either through your employer plan or individually, that allows for tax deductible contributions during your working years that grow tax-deferred until needed in retirement. They are invested in the products you choose within the portfolio offerings available to your account, which vary based on your employer. These kinds of plans are available in normal circumstances without penalty after age fifty-nine-and-one-half and

---

[17] Securities and Exchange Commission. "Traditional and Roth 401(k) plans." https://www.investor.gov/introduction-investing/retirement-plans/employer-sponsored-plans/traditional-roth-401k-plans.

must be accessed beginning at age seventy-and-one-half (with some exceptions for employees who are still actively working). The seventy-and-one-half age requirement is called a Required Minimum Distribution (RMD) with percentage of withdrawals determined by the IRS age tables.

IRA

An IRA may be either an individual retirement account you establish with a financial services company—such as a bank, brokerage firm, or mutual fund company—or an individual retirement annuity that's available through an insurance company.

Certain retirement plans, including a simplified employee pension (SEP) and a SIMPLE (Savings Incentive Match Plan for Employees of Small Employers) may be set up as IRAs, though they operate a little differently from those you set up yourself.

Earnings on investments in a traditional IRA are tax-deferred for as long as they stay in your account. When you take money out—which you can do without penalty when you turn fifty-nine-and-one-half and are required to begin doing once you turn seventy-and-one-half—your withdrawal is considered regular income so you'll owe income tax on the earnings at your current rate. If you deducted your contribution (traditional contributions), tax is due on your entire withdrawal. If you didn't (after-tax, or Roth, contributions), tax is due only on the portion that comes from earnings.

You can't contribute any additional amounts to a traditional IRA once you turn seventy, even if you're still working.[18]

---

[18] FINRA. "Individual Retirement Accounts."
http://www.finra.org/investors/individual-retirement-accounts

Roth IRA

Contributions to a Roth IRA are always made with after-tax income, but the earnings are tax-free if you follow the rules for withdrawals: You must be at least fifty-nine-and-one-half and your account must have been open at least five years. What's more, with a Roth IRA you're not required to withdraw your money at any age—you can pass the entire account on to your heirs if you choose. And you can continue to contribute to a Roth as long as you have earned income, no matter how old you are. Contribution levels for a Roth are the same as those for a traditional IRA. However, there are income restrictions associated with contributing to a Roth IRA. Both you and your spouse can each establish your own Roth IRAs.[19]

ETFs

Exchange-traded funds (ETFs) are SEC-registered investment companies that offer investors a way to pool their money in a fund that invests in stocks, bonds, or other assets. In return, investors receive an interest in the fund. Most ETFs are professionally managed by SEC-registered investment advisers. Some ETFs are passively-managed funds that seek to achieve the same return as a particular market index (often called index funds), while others are actively managed funds that buy or sell investments consistent with a stated investment objective.

ETFs are not mutual funds. But, they combine features of a mutual fund, which can only be purchased or redeemed at the end of each trading day at its NAV per share, with the ability to trade throughout the day on a national securities exchange at market prices. Before investing in an ETF, you should read its summary

---

[19] FINRA. "Individual Retirement Accounts."
http://www.finra.org/investors/individual-retirement-accounts

prospectus and its full prospectus, which provide detailed information on the ETF's investment objective, principal investment strategies, risks, costs, and historical performance (if any).[20]

Wrap Account

A wrap account is an investment account where a "wrapped" fee or fees cover all the management, brokerage, and administrative expenses for the account. The fee or fees are generally based on the total market value of the investment account.[21]

Income Plan

A written, structured document detailing the sources of income from all sources in retirement to include those structured from your personal retirement accounts as well as Social Security, pension, and all other fixed sources. It must include provision for inflation and spousal continuation as well. To be predictable, it must reflect structured, contractual sources of income.

Annuity

An annuity is a contract between you and an insurance company that requires the insurer to make payments to you, either immediately or in the future. You buy an annuity by making either a single payment or a series of payments. Similarly, your payout may come

---

[20] Securities and Exchange Commission. "Exchange-Traded Funds (ETFs)." https://www.sec.gov/fast-answers/answersetfhtm.html.

[21] Securities and Exchange Commission. "Wrap Account." https://www.investor.gov/additional-resources/general-resources/glossary/wrap-account.

from the insuring company either as one lump-sum payment or as a series of payments over time.[22]

Fixed Indexed Annuity

An example of a more robust definition found on an insurance company's website:

A fixed indexed annuity is a tax-deferred, long-term savings option that provides principal protection in a down market, as well as the opportunity for growth. It gives you more growth potential than a fixed annuity along with less risk and less potential return than a variable annuity.

Returns are based on the performance of an underlying index, such as the S&P 500® Composite Stock Price Index, a collection of 500 stocks intended to provide an opportunity for diversification and represent a broad segment of the market. While the benchmark index does follow the market, as an investor, your money is never directly exposed to the stock market.

Fixed annuities are contracts purchased from a life insurance company. They are designed for long-term retirement goals. Withdrawals are subject to income tax, and withdrawals before age fifty-nine-and-one-half may be subject to a 10 percent early withdrawal federal tax penalty. All guarantees and protections are subject to the claims-paying ability of the issuing insurance company.[23]

---

[22] Securities and Exchange Commission. "What Are Annuities?" https://www.investor.gov/introduction-investing/basics/investment-products/annuities.

[23] Nationwide. "What Is a Fixed Indexed Annuity?" https://www.nationwide.com/what-is-a-fixed-indexed-annuity.jsp.

Income Rider

An income rider is a contractual element that may be attached to a fixed indexed annuity for a fee. It is designed to provide a structured lifetime income for either a single or joint need at a specific yield to the client. These are often used in retirement due to the shifting focus from growth to yield the rider provides.

Sequence of Returns Risk

This is the effect on a retirement portfolio that either a rising or declining market has on the sustainability of providing a lifetime of income. Generally speaking, a positive market performance early in the retirement sequence (think 2009 until 2018) will result in a sustainable income. Conversely, a negative performing market (think 2001 or 2008) when first drawing income may result in the income being unsustainable.

4 Percent Rule

In 1994, a financial advisor named William Bengen offered an answer to this question: the "4 percent rule."

After analyzing historical financial data, Bengen concluded that a retiree with an investment portfolio split between stocks and bonds could "safely" withdraw 4 percent from that portfolio during the first year of retirement and follow up with inflation-adjusted withdrawals in subsequent years. In thirty years, there would still be money left over, his research showed.[24]

---

[24] FINRA. "What You Need to Know About the 4 Percent Rule."
http://www.finra.org/investors/what-you-need-know-about-4-percent-rule.

GAO

The U.S. Government Accountability Office (GAO) is an independent, nonpartisan agency that works for Congress. Often called the "congressional watchdog," GAO examines how taxpayer dollars are spent and provides Congress and federal agencies with objective, reliable information to help the government save money and work more efficiently.[25]

FRA

Full retirement age, or FRA, is the age at which a person may first become entitled to full or unreduced retirement benefits.[26]

Shoobie

The term given decades ago to the weekend beach visitors, arriving mostly by train. Shoobies came complete with their baskets of provisions that descended throughout the summer months to enjoy the Wildwood's beaches.

---

[25] Government Accountability Office. "About."
https://www.gao.gov/about/

[26] Social Security. "Retire Chart."
https://www.ssa.gov/planners/retire/retirechart.html

About the Author

A former displaced Pittsburgh steelworker, Roy Laux brings more than thirty years of experience in the investment and insurance industry to Synergy Group. Since 1988, he has helped thousands of retirees and pre-retirees develop successful retirement strategies through his simple, yet powerful, approach.

Roy holds his Series 6 and 63 securities licenses as well as life, health, and accident insurance licenses in Pennsylvania.

Roy has been a featured speaker for many local businesses and quoted in dozens of financial media outlets including CNBC, FoxNews, and Bankrate.com.

In his spare time, Roy enjoys spending his time with his family, particularly his eight grandchildren.

About Synergy Group

Founded in 1988, Synergy is an independent financial services firm that focuses on retirement. We serve clients throughout the Pennsylvania area. We pride ourselves in having developed our business by building trusting, respectful relationships with those we serve as clients. Our staff has a diverse array of licenses and specialties, which we use in our holistic approach to retirement strategies.

Jason Laux, Vice President

Jason has worked at The Synergy Group as an advisor and marketing coordinator for more than fourteen years, with a total of eighteen years of involvement in the financial services industry.

Jason holds a Bachelor of Arts from Pennsylvania State University, where graduated summa cum laude in advertising and public relations with a concentration in business and economics. An Investment Advisor Representative, Jason holds his Series 6, 63 and 65 licenses as well as life, health and accident insurance licenses in Pennsylvania.

Jason has conducted hundreds of financial workshops over the past ten-plus years. He has been featured in many media outlets, including Fox Business, MSNBC, and The Investor News.

Jason loves spending time with his wife, Danielle, as well as his four children: Aidan, Tyler, Colton, and Brielle.

Terry Judy, Senior Advisor

Terry came to Synergy Financial Group ten years ago after beginning his financial services career at the Great American Savings and Loan Association.

An Investment Advisor Representative, Terry has conducted hundreds of financial and retirement meetings over the years. He holds his Series 65 license as well as health, life, and accident insurance licenses in Pennsylvania.

Outside of the office, Terry serves on the board of the First Evangelical Free Church of McKeesport and is a member of the Advisory Board of the Champion Christian Family and Children's Center in Donegal, Pennsylvania.

Terry and his wife, Laura, enjoy rooting for Penguins hockey, traveling, and visiting with their grandchildren in the Harrisburg area.

Steve Ross, Advisor Support/Marketing Director

As advisor support and marketing director, Steve offers client and advisor support while also helping with retirement plan development and overseeing marketing operations.

Steve graduated from Point Park University and before he started a career in financial services, Steve worked in employee benefits and gained extensive marketing experience with a Fortune 500 company.

When Steve's not at the office, he likes traveling and exploring new places with his wife Erin and hanging out with his dog, Nala.

Contact Us

If the topics and information in this book rang true to you, please don't continue to go it alone on your retirement income planning. Give me and my associates at Synergy Group a call and find out more about "off-season" planning for retirement.

Roy Laux
The Synergy Group
1967 Lincoln Way
White Oak, PA 15131
Toll Free: 800-321-SYNERGY | Local: 412-673-7760
info@synergygroupinc.com

41850459R00068

Made in the USA
Middletown, DE
11 April 2019